THE COMPANY OF NEIGHBOURS:
REVITALIZING COMMUNITY THROUGH
ACTION-RESEARCH

The town of Hespeler in southwestern Ontario is an old industrial community that has lost its core manufacturing businesses, its municipal status, and its civic pride in the time since the end of the Korean War. In the early 1990s, Banks and Mangan implemented a community-development, action-research project designed to rebuild and revitalize the town. This book illustrates the success of local citizens in the revival of their community and the discovery of a nascent network of mutual support among neighbours.

The authors demonstrate how inquiry, education, and action-research can combine to form an effective model for engaged ethnographic analysis. Their application of narrative inquiry to community-based research is new, and their conclusion – that externally generated, imposed structure impedes community automony and responsibility – is well supported. The book significantly expands the established theoretical framework of action-research and offers an exciting alternative to existing models of community development.

The Company of Neighbours demonstrates a valuable approach for researchers, social workers, educators, and geographers in facilitating the collective efforts of people in local communities to shape the conditions of their own lives. With a new farmers' market, a museum in the renovated train station, youth programs, and an invigorated Business Improvement Association, Hespeler is well on its way to a new identity.

C. KENNETH BANKS is the director of the Family Service Institute in Toronto and an assistant professor of social work at the State University of New York, Buffalo.

J. MARSHALL MANGAN is an assistant professor of education at the University of Western Ontario.

C. KENNETH BANKS
AND
J. MARSHALL MANGAN

The Company of Neighbours: Revitalizing Community through Action-Research

UNIVERSITY OF TORONTO PRESS
Toronto Buffalo London

© University of Toronto Press Incorporated 1999
Toronto Buffalo London

ISBN 0-8020-0936-0 (cloth)
ISBN 0-8020-7905-9 (paper)

Canadian Cataloguing in Publication Data

Banks, C. Kenneth (Charles Kenneth), 1940–
  The company of neighbours: revitalizing community through action-research

  Includes bibliographical references and index.
  ISBN 0-8020-0936-0 (bound)   ISBN 0-8020-7905-9 (pbk.)

  1. Community development – Ontario – Hespeler – Case studies.
  2. Evaluation research (Social action programs) – Case studies.   3. Social
  service – Research – Ontario – Hespeler – Case studies.   4. Action research –
  Ontario – Hespeler – Case studies.   5. Hespeler (Ont.) – Social conditions.
  I. Mangan, John Marshall, 1947–   .   II. Title

  HN110.H47B36 1999   361.2'5   C99-930014-8

University of Toronto Press acknowledges the financial assistance to its
publishing program of the Canada Council for the Arts and the Ontario Arts
Council.

This book has been published with the help of a grant from the Humanities
and Social Sciences Federation of Canada, using funds provided by the
Social Sciences and Humanities Research Council of Canada.

Contents

Acknowledgments

The Company of Neighbours is a community-development project, an action-research project, a catalyst for change, a place for friends to meet, and a motivational force within its community. But most of all it is a spirit, an attitude, a determination not to let something vital and important fade away, but instead to make it stronger and richer. It has been made possible by the participation of a large number of people, most of whom are acknowledged within this text, but many of whom can never be acknowledged fully or formally.

Nevertheless, we must recognize the sources of assistance without whom we could not have begun or continued this endeavour. Bob Couchman supplied indispensable advice and encouragement during the various planning and proposal stages. The Donner Canadian Foundation provided initial funding to get the Company of Neighbours started. From 1995 to 1997, the Trillium Foundation provided funding to allow the project to continue. From September 1995 to the time of writing, the project was guided by a steering committee composed of the authors and a varying number of Hespeler residents, including Bill O'Krafka, Reg Prior, Archie Scott, Christine Boyle, Ken Boyle, Ken Buller, Russell Bygrave, John Gunther, John Jeffery, David Mitten, Elmer Schwartzentruber, and Joann Woods.

Gail Wideman served as administrator during the project's first three years and was instrumental in organizing the data collection and organization. Many Hespeler residents read and commented on early drafts of this manuscript. Rudi Czekalla, Alan Jeffrey, members of the Qualitative Methods Study Group (QualMS) at the University of Western Ontario, and three anonymous reviewers all provided helpful input on textual revisions. Lin Jie assisted us in preparing the index. But the person who most personifies the spirit of the Company of Neighbours, and who has been a bulwark throughout its progress, has been Joann Woods, who also served as secretary to the Great Hespeler Reunion. To all who have assisted in the preparation of this work, our thanks.

This book is dedicated to our spouses, Patricia Banks and Lynn Dunikowski, who provided encouragement and support to us during its preparation, and to the memory of John Jeffery, an exceptional individual, a wonderful teacher, and a resident of Hespeler who will be greatly missed.

C. Kenneth Banks
J. Marshall Mangan
January 1999

THE COMPANY OF NEIGHBOURS:
REVITALIZING COMMUNITY THROUGH
ACTION-RESEARCH

Introduction:
The Social Context

Across Canada at the close of the twentieth century, we are facing the withering of the welfare state (Couchman 1986; McQuaig 1993). The impact of diminished universal programs of health and social care, of lowered standards of living, and of disparities in the distribution of resources is exacerbated by the even more significant loss of our beliefs and assumptions regarding the notion of reciprocal obligation. Politicians are holding up their abdication of responsibility for vulnerable members of the population as an opportunity to ignite 'good old-fashioned' forms of community care. That care is supposed to be provided by an illusory army comprising family, friends, and volunteers, classified by some as 'the social sector' (see Drucker 1993). However, communities of the 1990s rarely possess the commonality of culture and overlapping of life activities that historically facilitated such neighbourly interactions and concern.

In addressing 'social deficits,' and in intervening to ameliorate the difficulties and incapacities of people, social workers have traditionally seen themselves as entering communities with programs of prescribed solutions, grounded in assumptions about needs that reflected the expertise of a particular planning body or group of professionals. Prominent social-work theorists have warned that, through these habits, social activists have lapsed into a state of inertia concerning issues of community building (see Campfens 1983).

Acknowledging this situation, some community social workers and researchers have begun to recognize the disintegration of the social safety net and of the institutions on which people have come to rely in times of stress related to finances, family, employment, and/or health. These workers have opted to break with traditional forms of community work and to explore new ways of identifying and fortifying extant community strengths, in order to facilitate *local* social change, appropriate to the particular community. The Company of Neighbours was founded to explore such new forms of community development.

The Company of Neighbours Research Project

The Company of Neighbours action-research project began in Hespeler, Ontario, in 1992, with Ken Banks as its principal investigator. He was joined in 1994 by Marshall Mangan as co-investigator. The project continues today as a locally managed, non-profit community association. Its three goals, as stated in the original funding proposal, were to use a qualitative-research approach to gather knowledge that would contribute to the understanding of informal and formal network relations; to help families identify and reinforce the indigenous strengthening components of their networks; and to demonstrate the efficacy and practicality of this research process as a social planning tool, to be employed by local people, in partnership with social workers, to further the efficient and effective use of those formal services that remain. The Company of Neighbours, as both a research endeavour and a community association, is predicated on a commitment to mutuality and to cooperative opportunities (see Banks and Mangan 1994). It is an attempt to move away from the kinds of outside-influenced, highly structured programs that have come to characterize much of the social work directed at individuals, families, and groups in the past.

The vision of the Company of Neighbours is to learn, through dialogue with communities, about the strengths and weaknesses of mutual-aid relations as they are engaged in by local people. We chose as the research site the small community of Hespeler, Ontario, which was, until the early 1970s, a busy industrial town in the agricultural heartland of southwestern Ontario. Urban regionalization changed all that. Since the textile, furniture, and appliance industries moved south for cheaper labour, or simply closed down, this once-thriving community has suffered visibly. The construction of the 401 highway in the 1950s isolated Hespeler from its traditional neighbouring communities of Galt and Preston. Regionalization removed services from the village core of Hespeler to more remote locations. An inadequate public transit system makes these core services difficult to reach from the town. The introduction of home-delivered mail in 1969 obviated the need for people to go downtown every day, and they stopped shopping there almost overnight.

The 401 put Hespeler within commuting distance of the ever-expanding metropolis of Toronto. As a bedroom community, it has seen new housing proliferate, inhabited by commuter-residents. Many of these people have felt that they have no time to explore, or to invest in, local traditions and long-standing relations.

In Hespeler, as elsewhere in Canada, this convergence of the old and the new, the rural and the post-industrial, has gone hand in hand with an attrition of state-sponsored urban amenities. The official rhetoric that has surrounded this attrition has suggested that governments expect an increase in the capacity for local personal autonomy. But where are people to find the resources to build and exercise this autonomy? Our research has been premised on the concept that a rediscovery of a collective local history, and the reconstruction of a meaningful, living community, can strengthen helping networks, as they have been reported to do for rural peoples in South America, Asia, and Africa (Chambers 1973; Freire 1993; Frideres 1993).

As social researchers, we designed the Company of Neighbours to be an *exploratory, descriptive, action-research project*. It is *exploratory* in that it embodies an unusual approach to community development, in which information gathering, consultation with community members, and facilitation of local initiatives take precedence over testing hypotheses or predesigned programs. Throughout the project, we have felt that we were exploring the limits of the possible more than implementing a preconceived plan. It is *descriptive* in that it places a heavy emphasis on locating and documenting the community's story, as told by local residents, and on describing, rather than prescribing, the course of events. It is an *action-research* project in that its intention from the beginning was to use the information gathered and the contacts made to facilitate reflective action for and within the community of Hespeler. We measure its outcomes as much in terms of the events that flowed from it as from the theoretical insights it has allowed us to generate.

Such exploratory projects require a research design that can be adapted to the process as it unfolds (see Corbin and Strauss 1990; Selltiz, Wrightsman, and Cook 1976). We have struggled to fashion an approach that would be rigorous yet remain flexible and responsive to developments. Through dialogue with the participants, the design has become progressively more focused as relevant issues emerged. At the same time, the project moved steadily from phases of information gathering and analysis to coordinated action and from being guided by the researchers to being led by local residents.

Organization of the Book

The purpose of this book is to share the authors' collective experiences as social workers, sociologists, researchers, educators, and participants in the story of the Company of Neighbours. That story reflects the unique circumstances of Hespeler, but we also hope that it may serve as an example of what may be accomplished by people who become involved with the kinds of processes that we describe. We intend the book for both academic and non-academic audiences, and we have made a conscious effort to keep it free of complex jargon and overly complicated theorizing. Nevertheless, as described in chapters 1 and 2, we base our action-research model on a carefully considered set of principles and a conscientious methodology. We have attempted to provide enough information about these topics to satisfy academic readers.

Our intention is that this book contribute to an understanding of community development processes in a number of ways. First, we hope that the people who live in Hespeler, and who accomplished so much through their participation in this project, will find their stories reflected accurately and in a validating and gratifying way. Second, we hope that this work will be a consciousness-developing experience for all readers, but especially for serious students of community development as a social-work endeavour and/or as a political process. We hope that students of community development, by reading this book, can become aware of their capacity to use investigative and organizational skills to identify local problems, define local solutions, and mobilize people and their resources so that they may act.

In chapter 1, we begin by outlining the guiding principles that form the theoretical framework of the project. We review the social and intellectual climate of postmodernism and the possibilities for an empirically grounded, engaged social science within the current milieu. For readers concerned, as we are, to locate clearly our theoretical foundations, we try to describe the general model of participatory research that we used – and which was clarified considerably for us during this project. We consider the specification of this model to be one of our contributions to the field and one of the most gratifying outcomes of the project.

In chapter 2 we begin by reviewing the roots of our field methods and the meanings of several key concepts. Our consideration of formal definitions sets the stage for an encounter in later chapters with the meanings of these concepts as embodied in the stories that we discovered through dialogue with our participants. We then describe in general terms the method of the project, including several innovative aspects that we believe were crucial to the success of the project in the long term.

Chapters 3, 4, and 5 are largely narrative accounts of project activities that emerged as a result of our identification of salient themes in the data and from our ongoing interactions and reflections with participants in the project. Together, these chapters tell the story of how the Company of Neighbours instigated a series of efforts that were enthusiastically embraced by the community and how that community subsequently took control of those efforts and saw them through to their culmination.

More specifically, chapter 3 examines the community's definition and delineation of social support networks and the ways in which those networks were socially constructed and maintained. Chapter 4 reviews the oral history of Hespeler and examines the development of 'a narrative community and a community narrative.' Chapter 5 describes the process through which our early explorations led to activities initiated and sustained by the community – activities that we could not have imagined in advance but which emerged as a gratifying and inspiring response to our approach.

We close with a relatively brief conclusion, in which we describe the most recent events around the Company of Neighbours, discuss our overall analysis and interpretation of the events as they unfolded, and describe what we see as the results of the mediating effects of our research.

Throughout the book we report on what has been said and done within our project and bring forward materials that we have woven into a narrative through dialogue with our participants. To a large extent, we attempt to let events, and the participants, speak for themselves in the central chapters, through excerpts from interviews, group meetings, source documents, and field notes. Where we feel it adds to the story being told, we offer an analysis of those events and statements. We comment, interpret, and theorize at key points as we perceive that there are possibilities of constructing meanings that need to be discussed in the community and beyond. Most important, however, we hope that readers will find here the fascinating story of people coming together, in a time of stress and dissolution, to reclaim their traditions and to seize control of their futures.

1

Community Action-Research
in the Postmodern Era

This book describes an effort to bring together social researchers, social workers, and the people with whom they work in a new set of relationships, intended to produce more fruitful, gratifying, and lasting results for everyone involved. In structuring those relationships, we found ourselves facing a profound set of challenges. We recognized that the welfare of the community in which we had chosen to work had to be our first priority. But we also wanted to develop methodological and theoretical grounds for our research, which would allow us to make lasting contributions to a knowledge base for similar efforts in the future. To do this, we felt that we had to recognize and describe the salient features of the social, political, economic, and intellectual contexts of North American life at the end of the twentieth century and to document the ways in which we have faced the demands and constraints imposed on us by those contexts. To this end, in this chapter we look at postmodernism, critiques of postmodernism, and fieldwork traditions that assisted us in formulating our own method of action-research.

Postmodernisms and the Postmodern Era

Many contemporary social theorists have described the current epoch as 'the postmodern era' or as 'the end of modernity' (see Giddens 1993; Jameson 1991; Lyotard 1984). It is an era that has already seen some profound reorientations in the social sciences. Those shifts are not 'merely academic,' however – they reflect some of the fundamental economic and social transformations that are under way in the non-academic world as well.

'Modernism' or 'the Modern era' is generally conceived of as covering about the last two to three hundred years of western history– the period from the Enlightenment, through the Industrial Revolution, the world wars, and the Cold War. The rise of secular rationalism and democratic capitalism as the dominant forms of socioeconomic organization, and their struggle with religious dogmatism, fascism, socialism, and communism, have been salient features of this period, alongside a rapid transformation of the scientific and technological environment. The social sciences arose as academic disciplines during this period, seeking initially to share the success of the physical sciences by adapting their methods to the study of humanity – though there have always been critical alternatives to the mainstream forms of 'scientific' sociology (see Bourdieu, Chamboredon, and Passeron 1991).

'Postmodernism' had early roots in artistic and intellectual movements of the 1920s and was prefigured by sociologists in the late 1950s (Mills 1959), but its real ascendancy began with the introduction of microcomputers and 'the Information Age' in the early 1980s. Among the economic changes that characterize postmodernism are the shift from a goods-based to an information-based economy, an emphasis on global competition, the virtual disappearance of traditional job trajectories, the fragmentation of mass markets into ever-smaller 'niche' markets, and the delivery of products to those niches via new media (see Drucker 1993). These trends find echoes in postmodern politics, which is characterized by the dominance of images over substance, the decline of conventional ideologies, the splintering of traditional party-based movements, and an increased questioning of established institutions (see Carroll 1992; Seidman 1991; Walker 1990).

While these changes in the social milieu have been occurring, the rise of a postmodernist sensibility within the academy has led many philosophers and social scientists to question the very foundations of the quest for a scientific understanding of society and to demand wider participation and greater diversity in the social-scientific enterprise. Drawing on decades of critical work in the sociology of knowledge (see Berger and Luckmann 1967; Bernstein 1983; Kuhn 1970; Mannheim 1952), postmodernist analyses have begun to challenge the authority of established scientific paradigms. More and more, the orthodox ways of interrogating and understanding the world have come to be seen as ways of maintaining traditional forms of power and privilege.

The challenge of postmodernism is reinforced by the critiques of historically disempowered groups: working classes, women, people of colour, and others who have not often found their experiences fully or accurately reflected in academic works (see Lather 1991; Richardson 1991). Those who have usually appeared in social-scientific writing only as 'objects' of research are increasingly demanding the right to be heard as 'subjects' – that is, as people with legitimate interests and valid points of view. They wish to speak of, by, and for themselves. Postmodern perspectives support their right to do so, as the authors of their own condition.

Postmodernism has thus spawned a number of theoretical and intellectual movements. It encompasses processes of social and economic restructuring that recognize the global context, while emphasizing the local and particular. It implies both different ways of thinking and different ways of acting, with implications for our material, political, and cultural environments.

Engaged Social Research

The rapidly shifting contexts described above place a heavy load on engaged forms of social research. By 'engaged,' we mean research that is concerned with social problems and which gets actively involved in addressing those problems (see Banks and Mangan 1993). Contemporary forms of social inquiry, if they are to remain relevant to current social problems, must respond to the postmodernist critiques of science. They must also answer to the growing ethical demands of the people whom they have so long claimed to serve. These challenges would be difficult enough to deal with in times of plenty, but now social science must fashion its responses within an environment in which resources grow increasingly scarce. Such a milieu threatens traditional ways of doing social science and social work, but it may also contain promising opportunities for useful forms of research, which will give people a chance to shape major aspects of their futures.

It was with a growing awareness of this shifting environment that the authors of this book and their colleagues began several years ago to formulate a research design for a project that came to be known as 'The Company of Neighbours' (see Banks and Mangan 1995; Banks and Wideman 1996). We worked together to fashion a style of sociological fieldwork and community development that could claim validity within the postmodern context but would also be useful to participants in the project. We realized that we could not simply adopt an existing, well-established research approach; we needed to seriously reconsider our model, and our methodology. The approach that evolved from our deliberations draws on a variety of critical traditions in social research and has been informed by the postmodernist critique of science, without totally accepting it.

Unlike most modernist scientists, we recognize that the logic of our research design, and the values implicit in it, interact in fundamental ways with our findings (Simon and Dippo 1986). This being the case, we feel that we are obliged to state 'up front,' and as clearly as possible, our initial working assumptions and commitments. We do not make the usual modernist claim that the strategy which we developed is something entirely 'new and improved,' which can be adopted holus-bolus by other researchers. Instead, it seeks to revive and combine certain minority traditions within social science, while we recognize that other inquiries will need to adapt this approach to their own setting and context. We feel, however, that this general strategy, sensitively applied within a program of action-oriented research, can help to ease the crises of understanding and the feelings of powerlessness within the communities in which we live and work.

Postmodernist Perspectives

We have alluded briefly to the theoretical perspectives of postmodernism but propose a more detailed examination of their qualities in order to establish the context in which we see ourselves working. At the same time, we must avoid reifying 'postmodernism' as any single, coherent paradigm. One of the most notable characteristics of a postmodern worldview is precisely its opposition to 'essentialist metanarratives' – that is, forms of discourse that claim to contain the one true way of understanding a given subject (see Lyotard 1984).

It is not our intention to adopt or impose any such characterization. Indeed, it would seem that postmodern theorizing is described more easily by allusions to what it is not than to what it is. Its texts are full of obituaries for conventional ways of doing research: 'Although many researchers do not seem to have heard the news, the traditional ways have lost their hegemony, if not their legitimacy, both theoretically and methodologically' (Mishler 1991, 260).

The primary target for such pronouncements has been the sociological program of positivism. Positivism has for so long been the orthodox way of doing social science that for many people it is invisible – it is equated with the discipline itself. Positivism is a means of applying the methods of the physical sciences to problems conceived in traditionally scientific ways: the 'discovery,' usually through rigorous experimental and survey methods, of the 'laws' of social functioning (see Burrell and Morgan 1979). Positivism claims both that the social reality is independent of individual experience and that its forms can be discovered and described in more-or-less objective and law-like terms. The dominant form of positivist theory in twentieth-century social science has been structural functionalism, which tends to view society as a large and complex machine, or as a kind of living organism that adapts to its environment in order to survive, grow, and reproduce.

To some extent, the strong forms of positivism and structural functionalism have become sufficiently unfashionable over the last quarter-century that they now find few public defenders. Even those who have set out to write 'In Defense of Positivist Research Paradigms' (Schrag 1992) have often ended up eulogizing it. Schrag concludes that positivism is now 'a philosophical view that has long been interred, and one I have no interest in resurrecting' (16). In spite of these concessions in the literature, however, the accepted mode of operation in many academic departments still grounds itself in the assumptions of a classical positivist model (see Gartrell and Gartrell 1996).

By contrast, postmodernist approaches reject ideas of a science devoted to uncovering the laws of an objective social reality. They tend to shun analyses based on myths of progress, unity, and convergence, in favour of multi-dimensional, multi-voiced descriptions of reality. Each such description is recognized as valuable in its own right, but also as having few grounds for asserting its superiority over other well-articulated versions, which may be grounded in other traditions. 'In postmodernism the self is neither unitary nor self-knowing; language is inextricably and deceptively ambiguous; and, reality is a funny kind of word' (Scheurich 1992, 3). This interpretation implies that there is no one right way of knowing something and instead that many valuable points of view are worth considering. In fact, many analysts prefer to speak of postmodernisms, in the plural, to emphasize the multiplicity of standpoints included in the perspective.

Thus postmodern critiques are not attacks only on positivism or on any particular methodology per se. They are primarily challenges to essentialist views of 'truth' and the officially approved procedures for gaining access to that truth. Those procedures have tended to privilege the particular skills and pronouncements of trained 'experts' over the discourses of 'ordinary' people – even when the ordinary people felt that they were being misrepresented (see Denzin 1992). The experts have tended to speak primarily to each other, in what Gouldner (1976) described as an 'elaborated speech variant.' They have displayed little concern about whether that speech variant was intelligible to the people who were the original sources of the scientists' 'data.' Those people – the 'objects' of the research – have not generally been considered an audience for the research reports. They were not expected to read what the experts thought of the conditions of their lives.

Postmodernisms question the grounds for such practices, maintaining that expert testimony has come to represent a particular intellectual world-view, which is conditioned by its own standpoint of dominant race, class, and gender. That standpoint has no valid claim to final authority over the ways in which people conduct their lives. Thus to some extent the postmodernist critiques of social science are a reaction against the suppression of personal and local forms of meaning in favour of an abstract concept of society. They point to the fact that orthodox social research has often had the effect of denying the lived reality and rationality of individuals and communities and that two centuries of modernist science generally has failed to produce a more just, peaceful, and habitable world (see John 1994). They thereby draw attention to the inextricable connections between knowledge and power and to the ways in which a quest for knowledge may also constitute a move to gain advantage over others (see Foucault 1980). They reveal the essential power differences between researchers and the people whom they re-search and the ways in which those power differences are based in a panoply of cultural disparities.

Such power relations are a particularly acute problem for what have come to be known as 'applied' forms of social science. Social work, education, and a wide range of therapeutic disciplines are dedicated to acting in the world as well as studying it. They are committed to an effort to achieve some form of social betterment through the treatment of individual needs. They have been called 'applied' sciences because, within the modernist paradigm, they were expected to leave formal research and theorizing to the 'pure' sciences. Their role was to apply the findings from sociology, psychology, economics, and so on in practical settings. This situation has traditionally relegated 'applied' disciplines to a sec-ondary status within the academy, where they have struggled to define for themselves a body of theory and a set of methods that are truly their own.

One of the reasons we prefer the term 'engaged' social science is to emphasize our engagement with the kinds of problems that are being experienced by real people, but without implying that by doing so we lower the validity of our own theory-building work. The postmodern recognition of 'objective science' as a futile dream puts a new responsibility on knowledge workers to examine and acknowledge their ethical and political commitments (see Lather 1991; 1986; Simon and Dippo 1986). But this effort not only to document what we see but also to act on our conclusions leads us to question some forms of the postmodernist critique.

Criticizing the Postmodernist Critique

For engaged social scientists, who are seeking a basis for social action as well as a theoretical understanding of society, there is an exciting sense of recognition, but also a cruel irony, in the confrontation with postmodernist thought (see Kemmis 1995). Engaged researchers are often in agreement with much of the critique of the rigid, dominating, and anti-human forms of modernist science. But the alternatives offered by postmodernist perspectives can lead to problems of practitioners' not being able to see the forest for the trees when confronted by pressing social dilemmas. The preoccupation of postmodernisms with issues of discourse analysis and the deconstruction of culture can lead to a complete dead end in terms of involvement with social needs and social causes (see Bauman 1992; McLaren 1994).

The postmodern context may, however, present opportunities for much-needed change within the social sciences. Recent feminist theorizing has in fact suggested a number of exciting alternatives that have influenced our thinking (see Haraway 1991; Lather 1991; Richardson 1991). These and other such bold reconsiderations of social inquiry have convinced us that research which retains a commitment to building locally based consensus and informed action, and which is willing to tackle the difficult ethical and methodological problems head on, may be capable of addressing postmodernist challenges to established forms of social science, while also providing some tangible results helpful to the participants. In the remainder of this chapter, we briefly review what we believe are the sources for such an alternative approach.

Interpretive Alternatives

For some, the antidote to the abstracted and impersonalized forms of positivist research lies within the interpretive paradigm of social science. Broadly speaking, this paradigm attempts to portray social phenomena from an 'insider's perspective.' There is now a large body of work in this tradition, which includes forms of ethnography, participant observation, and life-history research (for useful overviews see Burrell and Morgan 1979; VanManen 1990).

The strength of the interpretive paradigm lies in its recognition of the 'life-world' as a social construct of interrelated human beings, who are constantly creating and reproducing its meaning and structure. It recognizes every social setting as having its unique features, but also as being susceptible to an empathetic analysis, which can reveal its essential qualities. It begins from the premise that the understandings of participants in any social setting must be sympathetically examined and comprehended by anyone trying to understand their life-worlds. Max VanManen (1990) states that his version of 'human science' 'is interested in the human world *as we find it* in all its variegated aspects. Unlike research approaches in other social sciences which may make use of experimental or artificially created test situations, human science wishes to meet human beings – men, women, children – *there* where they are naturally engaged in their worlds ... The aim is to construct an animating, evocative description (text) of human actions, behaviors, intentions, and experiences as we meet them in the lifeworld' (18–19).

More radical forms of interpretive social science may strive only to represent the 'life-world' as completely as possible (without presenting an analysis). The grounds for such an endeavour are that a complete description is a sufficient contribution to a scientific understanding of cultures and subcultures that are not one's own and that any attempt to go beyond that is a form of imposition by the researcher. Describing one of his interpretive studies, George Willis (1991) says that 'the basic methodology, therefore, is simply to collect as many reports as possible of the phenomenological states of others and let these reports speak for themselves' (183).

Clearly, such a stance is quite different from that of a positivist social science and may be taken as almost its polar opposite. Where positivist science privileges the voice of the scientist, interpretive science of this type attempts to give primacy to the voice of the subject, by sympathetically reporting on his or her life-world. We feel that this is an essential starting point for any engaged social science, which must approach an understanding of social problems with a serious effort to 'get inside' those problems as people experience them personally and directly. Unfortunately, interpretive forms of social science do not provide much in the way of solid grounds for moving beyond description to positive action. As VanManen (1990) says clearly, 'Phenomenology does not problem solve' (22). By contrast, engaged social science has a clear commitment to an attempt to develop solutions, as well as understandings.

We are also troubled by what we see as an implicit claim to a kind of neutrality in approaches which claim that they are 'only' doing description. The claim of this type of interpretive social science to be merely reporting the perspectives of its subjects can become, in an ironic way, similar to the claim of positivism to be capable of some form of objective observation (see Habermas 1987). Phenomenological accounts acknowledge that they represent a particular human experience, but they also claim that there is an underlying essence to such experience. This assumption may serve to deny or disguise the influence of fundamental characteristics of the researchers. Authors writing from within the interpretive paradigm, like all writers, come from specific personal and cultural backgrounds, which are often markedly different from those being researched. Such differences need to be acknowledged and confronted.

Postmodernist approaches deny the possibility of any essentialist account of human experience, which would be true for all. Instead, the postmodernist perspective insists that all forms of discourse should recognize the limitations of their own locations. This implies a critique of traditional interpretive paradigms as well as of positivist forms of inquiry. Postmodernist stances recognize that even analyses of historical texts, interview transcripts, and mailed-out surveys are profoundly shaped by the structure of their phrasing, recording, and transcription (see Mishler 1991). The act of research itself – the process of interacting with research subjects – always affects participants in ways that should not be discounted or ignored. Differences of power and authority, as well as of knowledge and experience, condition every social exchange (see Foucault 1980).

Postmodernisms thus reject the logical possibility of a neutral account of society. The position of an engaged social science, as we see it, should be to recognize this impossibility and also to reject the *desirability* of a detached or uninvolved form of social inquiry. As engaged social scientists, we still harbour a deep desire to understand social phenomena in all their intricacies. But we also have a commitment to act, and to encourage others to act, on those understandings. We hope that our work can provide a resource that will allow for informed action, with the goal of addressing some of the problems identified by clients and research participants. The definition of those problems and the grounds for action will always be problematic, but it is pointless to deny the reality of people's pain and despair or to objectify their need to take action within their social context.

In saying this, we do not wish to pretend that the action orientation of engaged social sciences is not itself problematic at times. The ostensible values of the 'helping professions' can function in some contexts as a form of ideology that works to create relations of dominance and dependence (see Illich et al. 1977). At the same time, however, we engaged social scientists are liberated from some of the conundrums of modernist science precisely because a position of neutrality or detachment is *not* among our goals. Our commitment to constructive action leads us away from any essentialist, unitary way of knowing, whose aim might be the attainment of some decontextualized, eternal 'truth.' It leads instead towards ways of constructing knowledge that is local, practical, and open to revision yet still has validity as both scientific understanding and grounds for action. It supports a reflexive form of research in which investigators strive for self-understanding (as actors in the world) as well as social understanding (as observers). As we see in the next section, such goals resonate naturally with forms of action-research and community development and with some of the insights of narrative inquiry and critical pedagogy.

The Grounds of Action-Research

As we have seen, a critical postmodernist outlook discards as inadequate both positivist notions of óbjective truth and interpretive notions of neutral reportage. These two great traditions may be seen as the 'grand metanarratives' of social research in the modern era – the overarching 'stories' that provide the underlying sense behind the activity. It is just such encompassing metanarratives that postmodernisms seek to unsettle (see Lyotard 1984). The alternative to metanarrative may not only be found, however, in isolated, subjective forms of discourse, in which all are equal in their alienation. There may be another option: the creation of local consensus through informed, structured dialogue (see Habermas 1984; Freire 1993).

Recent reconsiderations of action-research models constitute the first signs of an emerging third path, a potential escape from the historical debates over the essential nature of truth, which date back at least to classical Greece. Such a third route is certainly overdue. The social-scientific 'paradigm wars' that have raged over the last several decades have often reflected an alternation between versions of truth as relative or as absolute, of social inquiry as completely alienated from, or completely immersed in, everyday life (Gage 1989). What is needed is a way of reconciling this conflict, not through some final victory by one vision over the other, but by the propagation of a productive dialectic between them (see Bernstein 1983; Goodson and Mangan 1996).

In our view, an engaged social science that is informed by, yet critical of, postmodern perspectives is active and involved in the participants' life-world but does not seek to create a unitary metanarrative. It strives to be self-consciously aware of its own position in the world that it is investigating and of the implications of that position. It pursues the creation of knowledge that is local and practical but which may have resonances important for others' understanding – knowledge that is useful primarily to the people involved and secondarily to the wider community that shares their concerns.

In developing our research strategy for the Company of Neighbours, we came to realize that the grounds for such a form of social science were unlikely to be found within the established traditions of social research, for the reasons given above. We were thus led to re-examine the 'minority traditions' of community organizing and adult education that have shaped our own forms of praxis to date. These minority traditions have by now long histories of inquiry and activism. In many ways, they are the precursors of postmodernist analytical positions, but they have never come to occupy centre stage in the academy. They derive from the basic recognition that many kinds of ignorance are imposed forms of social and political oppression and that a lack of skills and information prevents many dispossessed people from acting in their own defence. These minority traditions include forms of narrative inquiry, action-research, and critical adult education, which can open up the dialectical process of knowledge production.

In some ways, the history and genealogy of these traditions have meant that, until recently, their political positions and their action orientations have been worked out in more detail than their philosophical and epistemological grounds. Perhaps in response to the postmodernist challenge, however, more recent reviews of such grounds have begun to articulate a coherent basis for a form of social research that is socially involved but also scientifically relevant (see especially Winter 1987). A brief review of some of the alternative models of inquiry that have recently been put forward should suffice to provide examples of how this might be done.

Concepts of Provisional Knowledge and Tentative Truth

A number of philosophers and social scientists have attempted to address the dilemmas of a postmodernist form of social inquiry, some in very sophisticated terms. Jon Wagner (1993) has recently proposed what appears to be a rather simple answer, but one that opens up a number of productive possibilities. He suggests that the search for truth give way to an effort to identify and reduce specific areas of ignorance. At first, these endeavours seem to be simply two sides of the same coin; after all, any form of research that could reveal truth would automatically reduce ignorance. The difference, however, is that one can work on local areas of concern, in which one is aware of one's ignorance, *without* making a strong claim to be searching for an objective, eternal form of truth. 'Truth claims are framed to emphasize timelessness, anonymity, and independence from context and historical moment. Statements about ignorance, in contrast, are grounded in particular people, places, times, and contexts' (Wagner 1993, 18).

Efforts to reduce ignorance allow for forms of knowledge that seek primarily to be sufficient for the practical purposes at hand. Waiting for certainty, for truth, means waiting for ever. Acting on the basis of reduced ignorance, however, is acting in the here and now, but in a way that is better informed, more reflective, and potentially more effective than acting solely on common sense. The results of such action, and their effects on the social environment, then become the elements of improved social theory. Emphasizing the reduction of ignorance requires that we recognize our own areas of ignorance regarding the local context. We must also recognize our roles as actors in the very settings that we are examining, as interlopers, and as educators.

Introducing the concept of education at this point is fraught with dangers, because it has become freighted with connotations of oppression and indoctrination. State-mandated schooling, as the most prominent form of official education, has long been criticized for its role in reproducing social inequalities and political acquiescence (see, for example, Apple 1990; Bowles and Gintis 1976; Giroux 1981). Advertising campaigns, industrial training, and governmental opinion-shaping have all been called forms of 'education' by their apologists. What we have in mind, however, is not any of these one-way processes of information transmission, but something much closer to the concept of critical pedagogy (see Freire 1993). A postmodern, multivocal conception of socially constructed understanding prohibits any form of indoctrination or 'banking' education, in which knowledge is 'deposited' in passive recipients. It recognizes the role of researchers as learners, but also their obligation to share what they have learned. As Wagner (1993) says, 'Research is a form of learning, and research reporting a form of teaching' (21).

The research designs that we are in the process of fashioning attempt to combine forms of narrative inquiry, action-research, critical pedagogy, and community involvement, to produce an engaged social research that will reduce ignorance about specific parts of the social world, while simultaneously providing grounds for action in that world. We are certainly not in a position to prescribe a 'correct' method at this point, on either epistemological or practical grounds. Instead, we wish only to point to some of the resources that we have found useful in developing an approach which attempts to fuse inquiry, education, and action into a workable form of engaged ethnographic research. This review of practices of research concludes our discussion of philosophical premises and sets the stage for a detailed discussion of our own methods in chapter 2.

Contributory Fieldwork Traditions

Working within the framework that we have described, we have found that the fieldwork traditions of narrative inquiry, action-research, and critical pedagogy have provided us with essential guidance in formulating our interactions with those who have volunteered to participate in our project.

Narrative inquiry as a basic approach to social data is becoming increasingly popular (see Polkinghorne 1988). Some researchers assert that 'storying' is a fundamental way of knowing for all humans: Shank (1990), for instance, states flatly in his first chapter title that 'Knowledge Is Stories.' Whether or not one wishes to accept this radical position, clearly many people construct their experiences, and indeed their understanding of the world, around key stories, whether as myths, metaphors, or exemplars. The function of storytelling in various domains of human life has been well documented: religious narratives and traditional Native healing approaches are two familiar examples (see Darnell 1991; Rappaport and Simkins 1991). The therapeutic application of storytelling in family therapy has been explored by Michael White and David Epston (1990), who postulate that in 'storying' our experiences we give order and meaning to our lives. In the event that people experience life as problematic, one way of understanding the situation is that their dominant story has been taken over inaccurately and unsatisfactorily by others. The therapeutic solution is therefore to generate an alternative story that is satisfying to the teller and ultimately more successful in guiding his or her everyday actions.

Though we do not regard our community development efforts as therapy per se, there may be a parallel approach in which the community becomes the creator of its own distinctive collective narrative. Perhaps we can expand the therapeutic application of narrative exploration to strengthen diverse aspects of community, by recognizing and validating the group's interpretive framework. As Bruner (1984) says, 'narratives are not only structures of meaning but structures of power as well' (144). Indeed, David Flynn (1991) has suggested that there is such a thing as a 'community narrative,' a shared story that defines essential components of life and activity within that community.

Thus, by soliciting stories from our participants, by listening to stories told individually and in groups, we begin to perceive the community as it is seen by those who live there. And by fashioning new stories, new forms of community narrative, we begin to forge new meanings around which people can structure their lives. Thus the Company of Neighbours seeks to locate both a community narrative, or the story of the town as told by its inhabitants, and a narrative community, a new form of polity that can tell its own story, and thereby to fashion a different ending to that story through collaborative action.

In order for the retelling of a community narrative to be effective as a form of social change, however, it must be guided by a disciplined form of reflection and analysis, as found within the practices of *action-research*. This model of research now has a fairly long and well-established history within engaged forms of social inquiry such as social work (see Lees 1975), economic development (see Frideres 1993), and especially education (see Kemmis and McTaggart 1982). According to Carr and Kemmis (1986), there are 'three important characteristics of modern action research: its *participatory* character, its *democratic* impulse, and its *simultaneous contribution to social science and social change*' (163–4). Guided by these impulses, action-research has struggled to define a style of inquiry that bridges the gulf between researchers and researched and which prompt genuine positive change in the settings where it is used.

In pursuit of these goals, Carr and Kemmis recommend primarily ethnographic methods, especially the use of interviews, followed by reflective feedback sessions, at which researchers present their tentative analyses to participants for confirmation and comment. They suggest field methods that begin with a concentration on recording participants' stories – their understanding and interpretation of their social practices. They also recognize, however, the need to move beyond simply recording participants' knowledge to a process of challenging and developing that knowledge in pursuit of improved forms of social organization and behaviour.

Seen in this way, 'action research' is not a phrase in which a noun (research) is modified by an adjective (action). It is a phrase in which two nouns are linked in dialogical tension: Action/Research; or action-research. This is the type of action-and-research, research-as-action, that we are attempting to implement.

Like action-research, *critical pedagogy* and other versions of transformative adult education have been with us for some time. In the southern United States, for instance, Myles Horton helped to found the Highlander Schools in Tennessee some fifty years ago (see Horton 1990). Highlander Schools were devoted initially to providing a relevant education to dispossessed miners and trade-unionists and later became deeply involved in U.S. civil rights struggles. Horton and his colleagues pioneered many innovative approaches to popular education. For Horton, self-organizing politics and self-educating movements were the only way to craft a genuinely democratic, grassroots reformation of American society.

Canada had its own version of this movement, in the efforts of Father Moses Coady and his associates at St Francis Xavier University in Antigonish, Nova Scotia (see Armstrong 1977; Laidlaw 1971). Through the university's extension department, Coady and his supporters developed a program that put them in touch with thousands of people in rural communities and which offered both an analysis of their political and economic oppression and a solution in the form of cooperative businesses and credit unions. Today the Coady Institute is still involved in developmental adult education, but now with a much more international, global focus.

Horton and Coady moved adult education out of classrooms and focused it on immediate social and political problems, but their early work was still characterized by what might be called a 'missionary' attitude. Their efforts lacked a thoroughgoing critique of the social relationships implicit in traditional structures of teaching and learning. More recently, forms of committed and critical adult education have arisen that are informed by a deeper theoretical analysis. Most analysts trace the origin of these forms to the work of Paulo Freire, which began in Brazil in the early 1960s (see Freire 1973). Freire provided clear and passionate descriptions of a form of critical pedagogy that sought to eliminate the oppressive authority of teachers and replace it with a dialogue among equals, which recognized the worth of working people's experiential knowledge (Freire 1970). He gave specific examples of the ways in which basic literacy instruction could be reformulated to treat adult learners as active agents in their society and their polity.

Orlando Fals-Borda (1991) has described the ways in which this Latin-American stream of theory gave rise to a number of 'participatory action research' (PAR) projects. These efforts aimed at combining basic adult education with forms of indigenous community development and local self-education. He perhaps best sums up his integrative philosophy when he says that 'a sociologist, to achieve fulfilment as such, must be a good educator of the people and a good social worker and, vice versa, that an efficient social worker should be able to transfigure technical social assistance and become an expert in theory and practice, a good sociologist and a good educator of the people' (Fals-Borda 1991, 35).

Horton, Coady, Freire, and their followers thus developed styles of adult education and community organizing that managed to express the dignity and authority of voices not usually heard. Together with developments in the sociology of knowledge led by theorists such as Kuhn (1970), Berger and Luckmann (1967), and Foucault (1980), these practical efforts helped to ground the emergence of postmodernist approaches. The common thread running through their struggles is that their conceptions of truth, and of education, are essentially dialogical – i.e., built around dialogue among equals. Action-research and critical pedagogy reject the use of knowledge as a source of oppressive power. They deny the authority of researchers, teachers, and administrators unilaterally to articulate, and then impose, their versions of reality on the living knowledge of people who have less formal schooling than they. Instead, these minority traditions of engaged research have been striving for a form of learning that is a process of mutual aid and dialogical exchange.

Conclusion: The Future of Community Action-Research

In this chapter, we have tried to describe our basic philosophical commitments, as enacted through our research in the Company of Neighbours. As a postmodern outlook insists on the variety of social meanings, we are committed to giving voice to as many different views regarding the social reality of our research site as possible; however, we are also committed to helping forge a sufficient consensus to facilitate meaning-ful action on problems that are identified by the groups with which we work. We are struggling to bridge some of the gulfs that have long hampered the effectiveness of engaged social science as both science and social activism. We are trying to narrow the gaps between research and action, between the academy and the community, between ourselves as professional information-gatherers and others who are seeking the infor-mation that will give efficacy to their desires. We are seeking to replace the scientific metanarratives with both a community narrative and a narrative community that will express its own validity through its lived reality.

Through the process of designing and implementing our action-re-search programs, we are trying to locate forms of social action that do not require the sacrifice of individual dignity in the process of seeking, receiving, and offering neighbourly support. Such new forms are not only desirable on their own terms but may be required as a result of the steady erosion of the publicly supported safety net. As government-funded supports are withdrawn, participatory action-research can pro-vide ways of structuring an informed and productive community response, which may reduce the sometimes destructive dependence on welfare-state institutions.

Forms of engaged social research that combine inquiry, education, and action hold the potential of resolving some of the perennial dilemmas of social research and, in different ways, of social action and community development. Provided that it guards against becoming a new form of prescriptive dogma, engaged action-research can propagate a continuing dialectic that will identify and address key areas of theoretical ignorance and practical need. The methods of the Company of Neighbours attempt to convene theory and practice in one forum and to forge a kind of praxis that will be meaningful and productive for researchers and participants alike.

2

Forging a Collaborative
Research Strategy

In chapter 1, we laid out what we see as the fundamental challenges facing community-development research in the areas of analysis and practice and the ways in which our research designs attempt to address these challenges. In this chapter, we describe more specifically the program of action-research that we developed as a means of documenting the community narrative, and building a strong narrative community, within Hespeler. We start and end with neighbours as our unit of reference, but concepts of community and society shape the kinds of relationships that we are attempting to foster. What we envisioned as the goal of the Company of Neighbours was the nurturance of clusters of neighbours who would consult with each other and act in concert on issues that interested or concerned them.

Our notion of a 'narrative community,' discussed to some extent in the last chapter, is not a new concept but one that has been under-used in community-development research. It relies on the recognition that language is a social process, expressive of a set of internal relations. The relations between ideas depend to some extent on the relationships among people in a community and a society. Community life is influenced by the stories that are told about the community and by the way in which the parties to the narration become conscious, not only of material facts about communal life, but of feelings and attitudes towards the ideas that are shared (Flynn 1991). The Company of Neighbours facilitates opportunities to construct meaningful narrative insights within diverse segments of neighbourhoods and communities, and it incorporates narrative as a cental feature of its methodology. Our hope was that we could draw on such qualitative approaches in social science to identify local priorities and to locate groups that could share their stories. We could then develop an analysis and facilitate a constructive praxis in places where the 'doing' of community had been obstructed and stalled.

As an action-research project, the Company of Neighbours also had an obligation to address issues of social-scientific credibility, validity, and ethical practice. To some extent, what follows is a variation on the standard 'methodology chapter' of a sociological report; we describe the research context, including methods; the exploration and description phase of our research; and our gathering of data from other sources. However, we hope that it can also be read as a story of our own arrival and eventual acceptance into a community that we came to love and respect.

The Research Context

The research component of the Company of Neighbours was designed primarily by the authors of this volume, Ken Banks and Marshall Mangan, assisted by Gail Wideman and with frequent input from Hespelerites and academic colleagues. Our initial funding came from the private Donner Canadian Foundation, with some contributions from the Ontario Ministry of Community and Social Services and later funding from the Trillium Foundation (see Trillium Foundation 1995). The early phases of the project were administered by Wilfrid Laurier University, but, as was planned in our design, control of the project eventually passed to a board composed entirely of community members.

Throughout its lifetime, Ken Banks has headed the project. Trained as a sociologist and professional social worker, for the first three years of the project Banks was a member of the Faculty of Social Work at Wilfrid Laurier University. He is now director of the Family Service Institute in Toronto and teaches at the State University of New York, Buffalo. Marshall Mangan became involved with the project in 1992 as a methodological and systems-design consultant. He joined the research team as co-investigator in 1994. He is now assistant professor in the Faculty of Education at the University of Western Ontario. The administrative coordinator selected for the project was Gail Wideman. When hired in the summer of 1992, she was a recent graduate of the Wilfrid Laurier MSW program in community development. She is now a supervisor of seniors' programs for the city of Kitchener, Ontario.

We selected the community of Hespeler, Ontario, as the site for the Company of Neighbours because it involved a confluence of characteristics that coincided with our research interests. We describe the social and historical background of Hespeler in the next two chapters, but we provide here some context for its choice as the site of our research. First, it had been a successful industrial town until the 1960s but by 1992 had the appearance of a veritable ghost town in its downtown and old industrial sections. Because of its location at the crossroads of two major thorough-fares, Hespeler was being promoted as a bedroom community for the Greater Toronto area. As a result, the town was on the verge of developing into a centreless sprawl, on the northeast corner of what is now the city of Cambridge.

Many of the previous residents of Hespeler had departed with the jobs when the main industries closed down. Many of those who stayed had none of the skills required by the high-tech companies that began springing up around Cambridge in recent years. The remaining residents from the tight-knit social networks of the old community were joined in more or less the same geographical space by a new group of relatively rootless commuters. These more recent arrivals had bought inexpensive and conveniently located housing without much thought for community life.

We thus recognized Hespeler as a community in transition, in many ways typical of Canadian society as it moves into a new era. Within this milieu, we wanted to report what the local people identified as their community and what their aspirations were for community life. Based on those findings, we sought to facilitate local action towards achieving the progressive ideas that emerged through dialogue.

We based our approach to the community of Hespeler on our understandings of the social and historical context of community-development social work and of the area in which we were working. The central concern that we had identified was the development of a broadly based organizational capacity to act. In a world of global competition, in which the state is abandoning concern for the welfare of vulnerable people to local communities, people need to regenerate that capacity for neighbourly action (see Banks and Mangan 1996). To a large extent, the innate organizational skills of people acting in communities have been weakened or destroyed by decades of abuse at the hands of both private capital and the bureaucratized welfare state (see Saul 1995). Community collective action once took place spontaneously and was largely taken for granted. During the nineteenth century, when Hespeler was founded and developed, neighbours generally looked after each other 'naturally,' as much out of necessity as of choice. Over the next century, however, society became more urbanized and diverse, economic conditions changed rapidly, and North American economies went through a series of boom and bust cycles, culminating in the Great Depression of the 1930s.

In the wake of the Depression and the Second World War, the social-welfare state developed rapidly and began to intervene more frequently in the personal and social lives of its citizens. Whether this intervention was benign or was meant to stave off more serious political challenges to the established structures of capitalism is a subject of continuing debate (see, for example, Aronowitz 1983). Whatever its roots, however, one effect of the growing influence of welfare-state institutions was that many communities' capacity for spontaneous self-strengthening action was dissipated by the increasing provision and control of social services by the state (see Illich et al. 1977). The result has been that, in places such as Hespeler, local knowledge of how to cope with and change social conditions has diminished along with the influence of the older genera-tion. The Company of Neighbours thus sought to support the develop-ment of a narrative that would keep the elements of community vibrant and rebuild the capacity to act effectively.

Methods from the Margins: Reflexivity

The 'minority traditions' that shaped our research designs – action-research, narrative inquiry, and critical pedagogy – we described in general terms in chapter 1. To a large extent, we drew the field methods used during the exploratory and descriptive phases of the project from these and other established sources on qualitative and ethnographic research – especially the concepts of 'grounded theory' (Corbin and Strauss 1990; Glaser and Strauss 1967). However, our approach has also been strongly influenced by some of the recent methodological develop-ments for dealing with disadvantaged groups. Especially important were the kinds of feminist-oriented procedures known as 'methods from the margins,' as developed by Sandra Kirby and Kate McKenna (1989). One of their innovative techniques is the admonition that researchers should be reflexive in examining their own practices as well as those of their research participants. They suggest that one way of doing this is for researchers to examine and document their 'conceptual baggage,' in part by conducting a self-interview.

Following these suggestions, we interviewed each other in January 1993, regarding our hopes, expectations, and preconceptions on entering the project. A partial transcript of this interview presents some of our basic assumptions and attitudes towards the project as it began:

Marshall: I wonder if you could just sort of start at the beginning. I don't think we need a lot of historical background, but basically I would like to hear you talk about the goals and purposes of the Company of Neighbours project. What are you trying to find out? What are you trying to achieve?

Ken: I suppose one of the things that is a central focus is that we are doing an exploration of people's perceptions of what their helping networks are, and how these networks work for them. We're hoping to get them to look critically at those aspects of their social networks so that they look at what is working well, what is strengthening them, and what is not working well and what is weakening them. And then hopefully find some people through this process, build relationships in the community, get to know people, pass on knowledge that we have, and encourage them in seeking out new knowledge of how to see the value of the informal things that they do, as well as the formal things that they do to help themselves when they are – when any event is coming up in their lives where they want to go and be able to talk to someone, and get some support they are looking for. It's not just assistance. It may be a celebration, maybe a high point in their life. Who do you go to? Who are you going to call?

Marshall: You mentioned that one of the things that you want to try to do here is to start giving away the kind of expertise that universities used to guard carefully. I guess that raises a certain question of, what is in it for you? Or what is in it for other people who might be able to provide this sort of expertise, and sort of seed process, to get this stuff started? Why would you begin to give away what was previously closely guarded?

Ken: The whole research team has a commitment to this. For myself, in twenty-five years as a social worker and administrator working with all kinds of people ... I've seen people being more and more alienated and more isolated and lonely and separated from each other, and it's not really their choice. You see, government, the state, has had a very strong agenda to socialize people in the way that housing is set up, the way commercial shopping locally has changed, the way that transportation is set up, the way that we remove certain kinds of services, for youth in particular, but for other people as well. Where we used to congregate, where it was natural, we stopped funding that in the last 10–15 years. I saw it all dry up.

I was working in some of those places where that was happening, when to me concern for others very suddenly became not a priority. So you can't tell me that it wasn't there, it was there, and more encouragement for interaction and encouragements for mutuality existed in the beginning of my career, by far, than exists now. People know how to cooperate and do things mutually, they don't like being lonely. I think that social work and sociological research have contributed to, in shifts that I have seen in these fields, to the individualization and away from collective opportunities over the years, and many of us have fought to keep the mutuality in social work.

It has been at times a devastating fight, and a fight that we felt in the mid-eighties that we had lost. But there seems to be a resurgence now. And so my commitment is to mutuality, and to cooperative opportunities. And moving away from the kinds of outside-influenced, highly structured program approaches to doing things; including media, that separate us, that get us more and more sitting in our houses looking at our TV sets, and only getting out to deliver the kids to the arena or something. That wasn't the way it was in 1968, and not that 1968 was wonderful, but there was less of that forced individualism with its devastating outcomes.

Marshall: Yes ... But it seems to me behind all that is a very narrow concept of what self-interest is. I don't expect people – this is sort of more my conceptual baggage than yours – but I would never expect people necessarily to act altruistically, or act solely for the good of the community, against their own self-interests. But it seems to me that you can define your self-interests as being something a little broader than simply, say, the maximization of your own individual income. I have often wondered what people, for instance, would be willing to say they would pay for the security of being able to walk the streets at night, what would they be willing to give up to have some sort of sense of attachment to their community. My hunch is that they might be willing to give up quite a lot, and that people can have a genuine, and almost a material, interest in having a strong, secure community. It doesn't necessarily have to come at the cost of other goods.

This segment of the self-interview touches on some of the central purposes of the project and some of the ethical and political context within which we saw ourselves working. It also reveals the way in which we, as researchers, developed our own ideas in dialogue, much as we would do with Hespelerites once the project was in full swing.

With this bit of 'conceptual baggage' in place, we can begin to examine the details of the fieldwork methods used in our project.

Exploration and Description: Community Needs

Having clarified our goals for ourselves, located the community in which we were interested, and selected the research team, we set out to explore what issues were seen as being of outstanding interest by people in the community and who was considered to be knowledgeable about those matters. We started with two or three people in the community whom we had heard of in the process of selecting the site and obtaining sponsorship for the project. These first contacts were school principals, members of clergy, and social workers – people traditionally viewed as 'key informants' in ethnographic research. We asked them general questions about the area: What did they see as its greatest strengths and weaknesses? What did they see as the major issues of their community's life?

After explaining the goals and procedures of our project to the initial participants, we asked each key informant for names of three local people who shared their concerns on some of the major issues that we had discussed. We asked if we could use the informants' names in contacting these three people, and this was seldom a problem. Obtaining these contacts was the first step in recruiting our interviewers and the first of several instances in which the Company of Neighbours broke with traditional social-science procedures. Instead of using graduate students or university-trained interviewers exclusively to gather our data, we wanted to get local people involved in the process at the beginning. We wanted individuals who were known and trusted within the community, and we wished to recognize their contribution by both paying them for their work and involving them in designing and carrying out the fieldwork.

By the end of our discussions with the key informants, we had a general sense of what issues were being talked about in the community and who was thought to be knowledgable about them. Our intention was that the social networks of our interviewers would constitute our interview sample. Though we were not trying to construct a strictly representative sample, we thought about potential participants in terms of the diversity of their contacts in the community, as well as their interest in participating actively in the project.

We tried to find out where these people 'hung out' in the community and arranged to meet them there. If they were known to take their coffee break at a local restaurant, for instance, we went there and introduced ourselves to them. In this way, their friends were also able to hear our explanation of the project. Word of the Company of Neighbours began to spread, and meetings with potential participants were arranged through the auspices of mutual contacts.

Once we had made contact and had some informal discussion with potential participants, we presented them with a job description:

> We are looking for 5 people from the community of Hespeler to assist us in interviewing people they know, about their social networks. Social networks are comprised of family members, friends, neighbours, church and community groups that we turn to when we want someone to be there for us. Interview questions will focus on the links that we use to celebrate windfalls or survive setbacks in our lives.

The time commitment will be four half days of training at $30.00 per session ($120.00) to take place during the month of January 1993. Your training will include participating in the design of the questions you will be asking in the interviews. Each interviewer would be responsible to complete 20 interviews at $15.00 per interview ($300.00). There will be an additional nominal payment for data entry. The interview should take about 45 minutes. The interviews will be completed during the months of February through May.

The response was good, and we soon had a short list of candidates from which to select the five participants who would become our ears within the community.

The next task was to make sure that participating community members had their rights protected. As with all university-based research today, our procedures were examined by an ethical review committee. Where interviews were involved, potential interviewees had to be made aware that they could refuse to take part and could stop an interview at any point. We had to ensure that no potential participant felt coerced to take part in those activities of the project that involved confidentiality and privacy. To this end, we prepared letters of information describing the project. We distributed these letters to all participants, along with consent forms to be signed. We also attempted to discuss our goals and procedures in greater depth with as many of the participants as we possibly could.

The Company of Neighbours Research Project

Dear _____ :

I would like to request your participation in a research study of personal and community support networks. The study is conducted by Professor Kenneth Banks of Wilfrid Laurier University. The goal of 'The Company of Neighbours' research project is to contribute to the development of an understanding of how family members ask for and receive support from a variety of community resources. Your participation will assist us in identifying personal networks and encouraging their effective use in local neighbourhoods.

If you agree to participate please return the signed consent form to us and one of the project's research assistants will interview you. The interview will take about one hour and will be audio-taped. The only persons who will review the information that you share with this interviewer will be the three researchers and the research coordinator. The interviewer will stop the interview at any point that you ask and your participation is completely voluntary. When the tapes are transcribed no names or other identifying information will be used. Names will be coded and kept in a secure location. The tapes will be erased at the end of the study. If you sign in the place provided on the consent form, we will provide you with a summary of the research report when available.

All information regarding you and your family will be treated in a confidential manner. Further, the research team assures you that your participation will in no way affect your support from any public assistance program. We are not a government agency nor are we funded by any level of government. We do not believe that there are any risks related to your participation in the study.

If you have any questions about this interview, please call me, Dr. Ken Banks at [contact information here]. Thank you for your participation.

Sincerely,

C. Kenneth Banks, Ph.D.
Principal Investigator
'The Company of Neighbours' research project

Our concept of including our interviewers as active researchers soon raised another problem: though we had promised them confidentiality as informants, we recognized that they, as collaborators, might not wish to remain anonymous. As contributors to the research process, they were ethically entitled to take credit for its outcomes. This issue has arisen before in participatory action-research projects, and we decided to follow the path recommended by Shulman (1990): we approached the interviewers individually, late in the project, and asked for their preferences about being identified. We assured them that they would be given the opportunity to review drafts of any report in which they were identified by name and that nothing would be said publicly about their work without their approval. In the end, all the interviewers expressed a wish to be recognized.

The five people whom we selected as interviewers were Wayne Barradell, Ken Buller, Jen Fitzpatrick, Verna Reuyan, and Joann Woods. Wayne, in his late forties, runs a home-based computer-education and -consulting business, with his wife, Mary. Wayne provided valuable technical assistance to the project at various times. Ken Buller, aged around fifty, had bought several old factory and commercial buildings in the downtown area prior to our project's starting. Over the years, he has renovated and rented them successfully. Ken is fiercely independent and feels strongly about not wasting government money on public projects. As a self-governing endeavour, however, the Company of Neighbours was in fact different enough from other government-run social-work projects that Ken was willing to serve as the organization's treasurer for a year.

Jenny Fitzpatrick, in her mid-forties, was on the kitchen staff at the local high school. She seemed to see the interviews primarily as a job for pay and largely disengaged herself from the project when they were over. Verna, also in her mid-forties, had immigrated twenty-five years ago from the Philippines. She was studying in a nursing-assistant course at the local community college at the time she was recruited as an interviewer. Joann Woods, in her mid-thirties, is married with three children. She was working as a waitress when we met her. She is a descendant of one of Hespeler's founders and would go on to become the community association's coordinator and only paid employee.

In addition to these Hespelerites, Gail Wideman, Ken Banks, and graduate student Nancy Solomon from Wilfrid Laurier University conducted some interviews with people in the community. These people, and other participants who took part in group discussions, we identify by their first names, with their consent, wherever they appear in narratives or transcripts of group meetings. In reporting the private interviews, however, we identify neither the interviewer nor those who consented only to be interviewed, in order to protect their privacy. Because Ken Buller and Ken Banks both appear in our transcripts, we identify them as 'K. Banks' and 'K. Buller.'

Preparing for and Conducting Interviews

In order to be consistent with our ethical and analytical commitments, the design of the interview instrument needed to be a collective and collaborative project of the professional workers and the local interviewers. The professional workers tried to explain clearly why they were in the community and what broad goals they had in bringing the project to the community. Regular training and discussion meetings examined interview questions that could elicit answers which in turn would shed light on issues that the key informants and the interviewers agreed were priorities for the community. We then used the questions as a guideline to assist interviewers in gathering responses in an overall consistent way. As can be seen from the interview schedule below, we structured the questions to provide only a general framework for dialogue.

The interviewee should have the letter of information at least one day before the actual interview takes place. It may be a good idea to suggest that you need a place where you will not be interrupted for the interview. If this is not possible in the interviewee's home, you are welcome to use the site office (just call us to confirm the time).

The Company of Neighbours staff will give you a list of interviewees with whom you may set up a scheduled interview. Read over the letter of information with the Interviewee. Briefly summarize your knowledge of the project using the outline, including your reasons for participating. Ask if they have any questions. Note: The signed consent form must be delivered to the Company of Neighbours site office before the interview can take place.

At this time inform the interviewee that you have only about 45 minutes to complete the interview. Start and test the tape recorder. Press record and 'test 1-2-3,' rewind and play back. Rewind and begin interview. Press record.

State date, time, at the home of (*interviewee's full name*). 'You have voluntarily consented to participate in this interview, and have read and signed the consent form and agree to have the interview taped, is that correct?'

Background questions:

1. How long have you lived in Hespeler?
2. Who is in your family (living with you)? Do you have other family near by?
3. Are you employed right now? part-time? in school fulltime? (*If not employed*): What do you think your job prospects are? Do you think you'll work in Hespeler?

4. What is your age?
5. What is your level of education?

Now I'd like to talk to you about who you turn to when you need someone to be there for you in good times and in bad. I don't require names, I'd like to know what relation they are to you if they are family, or if they are neighbours, or acquaintances or professionals or agencies.

1. Think back to a time when you had good news to celebrate (e.g. you won a car, you got a job). Who did you call first? Who did you turn to next?
2. Think back to a time when you had a financial crisis (your car has broken down and you need it for work, the cost of the re- pairs are more than you have). Who do you call first? Was this successful? If not, how did this make you feel? Where did you go next?
3. Who can you count on to talk about problems that are related to your school or workplace? (i.e. you're worried about school work or you don't get along with a co-worker)? How do you feel about asking for help?
4. Do you think of Hespeler as a friendly place? Why or why not?
5. Do you have a lot of friends to talk to? Do you find it easy to talk to friends? What makes it easy/hard?
6. Do you find it easy to talk to family? What makes it easy/hard?
7. Do you count on your friends when you need help? Your fam- ily? Who do you turn to first? Do most of your friends feel the same way?
8. We are studying informal and formal networks. Informal networks are your family and friends who help you out. Formal networks are professional services such as doctors, social workers, teachers etc. How do you feel about using professional services? Would you use them if you were in a crisis?
9. Have you ever needed such a service but it wasn't available in Hespeler?
10. Do you find it easy to talk to professionals? What makes it easy/ hard?
11. Do you have any ideas for how to improve the community of Hespeler for young people? At what level would you be willing to be involved if other people felt the same way?

With the framework for the interviews in place, we had to compile lists of interviewees. A key aspect of our approach to Hespeler was our commitment to investigate local support networks by allowing the interviewers to define those networks and to select participants from those within them. This put the task of defining the network members into the hands of the interviewers. Also, for a discussion of topics as sensitive as those in which we were interested, this approach offered the great advantage of a kind of pre-established rapport between interviewers and their subjects. We accepted the risk that our interviewers might not be as 'detached' or as 'professional' in their interview technique as trained social scientists might be, for we felt that the payoff in terms of honesty and intimacy would make the process worthwhile. Eventually, about fifteen to twenty interviews were scheduled for each of the five interviewers, plus the interviews done by Ken, Gail, and Nancy. A total of about 160 interviews took place.

Training for the interviewers required a delicate balance among several vital elements: encouragement of 'natural' social skills and the free-flowing conversation that takes place among friends; maintenance of sufficient distance to avoid gossiping or prying and to stay 'on task'; and the need to follow the general outline of questions that we had agreed to ask, while allowing for open-ended responses. Interviewers also had to learn and practise a few skills in order to recognize and avoid intrusiveness. Interviewers had to be ready to stop and hear surprising details that might be salient but were unsolicited. Confidentiality of the interview contents was consistently emphasized. Interviews were generally forty-five minutes to an hour in length and were taped and then transcribed.

We had four training sessions, which included activities with a number of university researchers. We then reviewed those sessions and focused on areas that were still not clear. Ken's field notes reflect this process:

We began by recapping the sessions, and 1) talking about being familiar with the purpose of the research, yet not having to have all the answers, in fact encouraging people to call us here (at the site office) for more information; 2) the fact that confidentiality is for life; 3) that it is important that the questions be used as guidelines only, that we need to develop the questions with prompts, such as, 'how does this make you feel?' 'what did you think about that?' and 'what did you do next?'; and 4) the interview is in fact a relationship, that requires that you be honest about your role and be sensitive to 'where the person is at'; e.g.: are the questions you are raising causing discomfort? If so, 'do you want to stop?' or 'is there something you want to say about that?' Or if it is apparent that there is an issue that must be dealt with, 'here is a number you can call.'

Once the actual interview process began, we conducted regular reviews of the interviewers' technique. These took the form of the professional team members listening to substantial portions of the taped interview. They then commented on what they saw as strengths and weaknesses of the interview, in light of how the interviewers and team members agreed they should generally go. Our field notes report:

Marilyn went over some questions they (the respondents) might have, e.g. 'Why interview me?' 'Why are you involved?' 'What's in it for me?' and 'Why Hespeler?' The group had good answers to these questions, indicating that they had done a fair bit of thinking around the project.

Next we walked through an interview, starting with the letter of consent. Ken described how the role-play we had done (Ken's and Gail's) helped us to see where we needed to improve how questions were done. For example, we saw that it was important to be able to say early on that for any more information they should call the office. Otherwise the interview would tend to drift too much, with the interviewer being asked all the questions. Marshall suggested that paraphrasing responses seems to encourage people to talk more.

Marshall went over the general questions that we wanted to ask. The summary question as we had it was: In an ideal world, what changes would we make to the supports available in Hespeler? Grant (student) pointed out that in an ideal world no supports would be necessary. Grant and Jen came up with 'If you had the opportunity to make any changes in Hespeler what would they be?' Great meeting!

After some experience, we came to realize that reviews were best done within three to five days of the interview. Such a procedure allowed participants to pick up errors and address any misconceptions that the interviewer may have. It also forced the project team to process the data while they were still new and salient.

The whole team met every week to discuss how things were going. Where interview questions seemed not be getting at the intended issues, they were replaced. When unexpected themes emerged, they were shared and noted by all. This is where the reflexivity that became so important in the process came into play: as we collectively learned how to improve the process, we made changes.

Because we wanted to build as complete an ethnographic database as possible, we did not restrict ourselves to interview data alone. On the contrary, we gathered information about the Hespeler scene from as many different sources as possible. Ken, Marshall, Gail, and Joann regularly kept field notes (describing events that had taken place and discussions they had had), as well as reflective notes (in which the meanings of recent events were explored and theorized and questions about or reactions to research initiatives were recorded). Partly at the behest of some of the senior citizens and their families, we conducted a series of video-taped interviews recording some of the 'old boys'' versions of the town's oral history. As group meetings with participants became more common, we began to keep notes and minutes, as well as audio and video recordings. As it turned out, these group-meeting records became in some ways more useful than the interview transcripts.

The records of interviews, discussions, and the reflections of the investigators were considered confidential data collected by the project, but there were other important public sources of information: press clippings, artefacts, books, newspapers, posters, photographs, and other memorabilia that participants began spontaneously to bring to the Company of Neighbours office. Each of these items added to our knowledge of the town's history, not only directly but also through the tales they inspired people to tell us. Some of these materials, such as locally written histories and the newsletters of the Dominion Worsted and Woollens plant, attracted so much attention that the project began to sell reprints as a fund-raising device – one of the earliest examples of 'action' arising from our research activities.

While data collection was still going on, we designed and implemented a computerized data-management system. We elected to build our procedures around a general-purpose database management system called DataPerfect, though a specialized program such as the Ethnograph might have done as well for this purpose (see Mangan 1994). We wanted to be able to divide the interviews as transcribed into quotation-sized 'bites' of information, which could be coded according to themes that appeared in the transcripts. We then assigned the segments keywords from a list developed by the research team in conference with interviewees. This process is conceptually like using different-coloured index cards or 'cutting and pasting' sheets of paper containing different categories of information.

The ideas behind the data management we drew largely from 'grounded theory' (Corbin and Strauss 1990) and from guidelines suggested in

Renata Tesch's work (Tesch 1990a; 1990b). By sorting the masses of interview data according to keywords and refining the themes that began to emerge, we drew agendas for community action from the data, not from the imaginations or preconceptions of the professional staff or sponsors. Theories about what was happening in the community and what should be done about it came from a diverse sampling of community sources. The theorizing was done dialogically by the interviewing team, the local community members, and the academic workers. These ideas in turn were checked and verified in the reflexive stage of the project, which we describe next.

Reflexivity and Ongoing Feedback

The locally recruited interviewers quickly came to know a great deal about the project. They helped to articulate the fundamental issues and to design the question guidelines. To some extent, they constituted an elite group in the project, as they had selected the research population and had become skilled in interviewing. When they gathered each week in the evening to discuss the quality of the interview experience, the project provided dinner or a snack, for we found that sharing a meal was a good way to get to know colleagues while focusing on a task. Within a few weeks, the interviewers felt confident in making suggestions as to how the data-gathering should proceed, as shown in this transcript from a 1993 meeting.

K. Banks: What I'm saying is, we're not coming in as teaching or telling, we're doing some of that, you know, the group techniques, the interview techniques, that kind of thing; we (academics) do teach and talk about that, and you pick it up and you go out and use it. But also, when you come in and say, 'This is working, this isn't working, this is a flaw with what we're doing,' that is as much you teaching us as us teaching you. It is an equal balance.
Verna: Are you going to be listening to those tapes for stuff that you perceive, for information sort of between the lines?
Gail: That's why this meeting is so important, because you have that information, some of it, a lot of it is stuff that's happened before and after the interview, or even just your sense of the interview because you were there. For example, some emotions we can detect from the voice on the tape, but much of it we won't be able to get unless you tell us.

The group talked about what questions elicited appropriate answers and what questions seemed to miss the point intended. From time to time, difficult ethical problems emerged as shown in the following excerpt:

Wayne: A woman was telling me a story about how she was afraid for her safety, but she didn't want it on the tape, and she didn't want it typed up, and she didn't want it written anywhere. But I think it's important to talk about it, and sort of give a scenario around why this woman did not feel safe.

K. Banks: So you could talk about it here, and it wouldn't be related to any interview necessarily.

K. Buller: I've only interviewed two women, but in both cases safety was a very strong factor, and it comes out very quickly. And they don't want to talk about it. 'How do you feel?', they don't want to talk about it. But turn the tape off, and they'll talk about it. They'll tell you anything you want to know.

Clearly, these interviewers had to respect their respondents' desire for confidentiality, yet we felt that a major issue was being raised – important for both the individuals involved and for the community. We decided that interviewers should let the people disclosing such information know that help was available, that we would know where to get that help, but that we would not try to provide that help directly and could not force them to seek it.

A commitment to reflexivity requires openness and flexibility, even in the areas where we may feel that we have some expertise. Local meanings count heavily as we try to reduce our 'areas of ignorance' regarding local conditions (see chapter 1, above). Such local meanings may not always persevere as we explore them in greater depth, but they must always be the starting point. Reflexivity also means that we come back to the same issue in different contexts. Over the life of the project, we changed and grew through our interviews, discussions, and writing, as well as through theorizing about the process.

People with very different backgrounds and views came to like and respect each other during this process. The interviewers may not have changed their views substantially, but they learned how to engage in dialogue about their different views, without hurting each other or being hurt themselves. The interviewers' group was still meeting every three or four months for chicken wings and beer, two years after its main task was completed. Members clearly felt that they 'owned' a chunk of the project and were quick to tell the team if we were missing the point in any of our continuing activities. As the project matured, and directorial authority was transferred to community members, several of the interviewers volunteered for the new association's steering committee. Joann Woods went on to become the office administrator, a paid, part-time position.

Gathering Data from Other Sources

While we were doing the interviews, we also began to gather data on life in Hespeler from a number of other sources. We discussed our impressions of Hespeler, and of the research process, at team meetings, which might include any number of the professional staff and the interviewers. We tape-recorded these sessions whenever possible. We kept field notes, which were typed into the computer regularly, if not daily. We spent time in local restaurants and at our site office, chatting informally with local residents and recording what we learned.

We discovered the centrality of the Canadian Legion Hall and the three downtown pubs – the Barking Fish, Ernie's Roadhouse, and The Olde Hespeler – to the social structure of the town. The consumption of chicken wings and beer in these locales was, we soon recognized, one of the key rituals of local planning and communication. To our gratification, the Company of Neighbours' storefront office on Queen Street, the main street of the old town, also became a gathering place. We listened carefully as people came in to tell us stories based on knowledge of recent events and of ways of seeing Hespeler from a local perspective on the community over time. We also began to structure several reflexive groups, whose meetings allowed us to discuss our initial impressions and to expand and enrich our store of data. We review the work of the two main groups to close the chapter.

The History Group

Over several months we got to know a half-dozen or more regular storytellers, who shared their tales with us, and gained from each other as well. Beginning with these storytellers, we formed what we came to call the 'History Group,' and we started to tape-record their meetings. One of the team-meeting transcripts recalls how this group came to be structured:

K. Banks: One thing that's going to be coming up in the next two or three weeks is: we've run into so many people interested in the history of Hespeler, that we're starting to get pictures, artwork, photographs, the people talking about the Old Boys' Reunion. So I talked to a handful of people about, well, what if we just asked a handful of other people they know that have shared the same interest in the research as you, and would they bring their stuff with them? And just set it up here and share it around and talk about the history, maybe on the tape, and then do a transcription of the tape, and then share it with everybody, and then it's not lost. And then also, if the group wants to do more, maybe get together again, we're not going to guide them, we're not going to give any input, other than to tell them about each other and maybe provide them with a place to meet, and help them meet.

People who did not choose to be part of the one-on-one interview process would nevertheless sometimes come to History Group meetings and talk on tape for hours with four to six people around the table. They began to bring in memorabilia: pictures of people in sports teams, at company picnics, and in downtown businesses, as well as old newspapers and written monographs of stories about the town. We put these items up on the walls and organized many of them in three-ring binders, so that people could drop in to add names to lists on the captions of group pictures. Besides the good times that were shared during these meetings, the collection soon attained some significance. Even the municipal archivist once came and waxed envious over the collection, and organizations such as the Legion bequeathed important records to the keeping of the History Group.

In meetings and activities such as those of the History Group, we were able, through a historical perspective, to check our interview data, and our interpretation of those data, against the group narrative that touched on many of the same issues. This process sometimes raised issues that did not surface in the interview data, as well as confirming issues that were featured there.

Initially, the History Group was a response to an expressed need within the community. As it grew and became more active, however, it became more central to both the organization and the activities of the Company of Neighbours. It comprised primarily senior citizens, whose own memories and collections of artefacts constituted a significant oral and documentary history of Hespeler. The activities of the History Group came to be so significant that we devote the next chapter to them. They eventually convinced us to facilitate the largest community-organization effort to come out of the Company of Neighbours – a revival of what was once called the 'Old Boys' Reunion,' but which became the Great Hespeler Reunion of 1996 (see chapter 5).

Interviewees' Group

We had planned from the start to invite our interviewees to gather and comment on our organization and interpretation of the interview data. At the end of the first year we held a 'thank you' dinner for all those whom we had interviewed as well as for our interviewers and some members of the History Group. There we talked about the project and what we were finding out. In the meeting we asked people to sign a book if they were interested in gathering at our office to talk about what themes we were finding in interpreting the data. Of the sixty-seven who attended the dinner, thirty-four signed the book, and ten to twelve actually came out to the meetings.

What we have done is less of a follow-through than planned with the interviewees' group and more work with the History Group and other action groups. This shift reflects our finding that a balance between the interview data and the input from the action-oriented reflexive groups works better than the sole emphasis on more individual-interview data that we had originally planned.

We originally thought that we would form groups from interviewees as they identified community needs from reflecting on the data. According to the action-research model often employed in other settings, a plan of action usually arises directly from the feedback sessions organized by the researchers (see Carr and Kemmis 1986). However, in Hespeler, we discovered that there was little enthusiasm for this approach. What did start to happen, almost imperceptibly, was that groups which had formed around common interests started to ask members of the Company of Neighbours for advice on how to organize or how to get what they wanted. We were most useful to them in providing know-how and resources so that they could do it themselves. Youths hanging out in the park, for instance, had already formed a band, but they needed a place to practice and for their friends to listen to 'their' music. Women in a new church congregation committed to providing community service asked for help in organizing a support group for unemployed women, a clothing depot, and an emergency food cupboard. Schools wanted older people to talk to students about the history of the town.

We found that we were gradually becoming more like brokers or facilitators for community action, rather than organizers or experts, and that we had been shown the way to accomplish this goal by the community itself. This was in many ways a vindication of our fundamental commitment to remaining non-directive in our interaction with the residents. As we came to realize, people often know how to associate in purposeful but informal ways within their communities. Such purposeful associations contribute to the maintenance of neighbourhoods and personal networks, though they may have little relevance to the larger society. Our project showed us that these local ways, if carefully nurtured, can gain new life and energy when it comes time to organize new initiatives. In the next three chapters, we present the stories of how participants in the Company of Neighbours came to identify (chapter 3), engage with (chapter 4), and act on (chapter 5) the central issues of their community.

3

Emergent Themes in the Community Narrative

We have now established the principles undergirding our approach to the study of community in Hespeler and described the methods that evolved from those principles. Our critique of postmodernism suggests that concern with understanding the 'life-worlds' of Hespeler's residents would be a starting point for our analysis but that we wished to move beyond an analysis of their words and into the world of action. We emphasized that we wished, rather than indulging in the construction of 'grand theory' (see Mills 1959), to concentrate on hearing Hespeler's many stories and the story of the community as a whole. Drawing on that community narrative, we might then begin the process of locating and addressing particular areas where a new perspective on local problems would provide for fresh forms of social action. To use Wagner's (1993) terms, we were trying to locate specific 'areas of ignorance' (but not in a pejorative sense) in the community of Hespeler, particularly regarding the construction and maintenance of mutual aid and neighbourly relations. Our findings, described in this chapter, led us to redefine our own concepts of community education, action-research, community, and mutual aid.

Context

In this chapter we begin to report the results of our collaborative action-research. Our open-ended interview process, though flexible, was none the less shaped by a collaboratively developed set of questions and themes. Those themes guided our early investigations into the attitudes and concerns of Hespeler's residents. There was a clear focus on community-building and mutual support, but we also made every effort to remain open to the possibility of discovering unanticipated nuances, and areas of interest within Hespeler, that were different from those with which we began.

Our use of local interviewers, talking for the most part to people they knew, resulted in an atmosphere of trust and rapport, which revealed many poignant stories of neighbourly relations. At the same time, by examining the transcripts, by talking reflectively with our research teams, and by meeting both formally and informally with various self-organized groups, we began to realize that some of the central concerns that we brought to our research, and some of the meanings associated with important concepts, were not entirely consistent with those of our participants. This discovery gave us pause on a number of occasions. It led us to explore the ways in which mutuality was construed within this living community and to redefine the concepts in light of these findings.

We found that our research program necessitated careful listening and interpretation of people's responses, both within our group of academic researchers and in dialogue with our participants. We found ourselves drawn into frequent discussions and debates, whether planned or not, over the definitions of key terms, many of which have been used in social-scientific research for years, with varying connotations and levels of clarity.

The process of working through the meanings of our initial investigations led us eventually to a different form of organizational structure, and a different set of activities, than we might have anticipated before entering the community. As we have consistently emphasized, however, the research aspect of the Company of Neighbours was an open-ended process of discovery, description, and exploration. Its primary commitment as an action project was not to any preconceived concept of community social work, but rather to a process of organizing and consciousness-raising, aimed at helping people achieve their own goals through dialogue and collaborative action.

Dialogical Development of Analytical Categories

As described above in chapter 2, the local interviewers formed a reflexive group, with which we conducted regular dialogues in order to identify key concepts, and to interpret their meanings for the study. We focused on family members in our initial interview-based inquiries; we then moved on to exploring people's interactions with and in institutions and groups. This gave us an opportunity to examine three central phenomena: the importance of local interpretations of central concepts in action-research and community development and the contrasts with more formal definitions; what people identified and defined as their social supports; and how people used groups and institutions to organize basic social tasks.

These organizing themes were defined only loosely at the beginning, but our qualitative approach allowed us to shape the process more clearly as the meanings of local activity were interpreted to us. Slowly, the articulation of socially constructed forms of mutual aid began to emerge.

The Importance of Local Interpretations

We demonstrate the approach that we used to draw out and report the social construction of meaning at the local level in the following texts. These excerpts from the discussions held among members of the university-based research team and the community-based interviewers' group reveal the explication of key terms. For comparison, we later consider some of the more formal definitions of concepts such as 'community' and 'society' taken from the academic literature. Finally, we move on to the lived, but often implicit definitions of concepts such as 'community' and 'social support,' as revealed through the stories told by interviewees.

One of the first places in which we discovered differences between academic and local meanings related to one of our central concepts – 'network':

K. Banks: We talk about networks a lot in the project, and what you interviewers talk about isn't family, but networks, and yet you say that 'network' isn't a word you'd ever use for that. Until you got involved in this project, you never thought about the social networks each of us had, and Wayne I think, was talking about 'family circles.'

Wayne: That's the kind of thing I think you were talking about. And for high-tech, sociological purposes, you could call it a network, but a family circle is that, plus it's more.

K. Buller: Networking sounds businesslike and rational, mathematical, like a grid. Network isn't the same thing as family, the way you're talking about it, because family the way you're talking about it is like network, only it's more ...

Ed: It's more the personalization.

K. Banks: But there's a lot of it you wouldn't call family, like, in your [Ed and Doris's] family restaurant, anybody, if the staff's busy, they get up to pour the coffee. That's not exactly family, but it is a warm sense of community, of belonging.

Wayne: They always made people feel like they were part of the family at Mum's Restaurant.
Doris: They felt at home.
K. Banks: So family is something that makes you feel 'at home,' even if it's just neighbourhood.
Doris: Home away from home.

Thus, though there was a concept of family circles within Hespeler, it was too loose and personal for most residents to associate it with 'networks.'

There was also a sense that perhaps a more formal social structure had prevailed in Hespeler's past. Local history was central to some of the older participants in the Company of Neighbours, but its importance to current social networks was not always recognized by the interviewers:

K. Banks: It's been coming up so often in the last six weeks: this fascination with, and great knowledge of, the history of this place.
K. Buller: I understand the interest of it, but I don't understand how it fits with people's networks.
Gail: Well, for one thing, people are saying that there aren't any networks any more, that there were at one time. So we can get people talking about what started those networks.

Beliefs and understandings that the researchers held as given had to be addressed and made consciously problematic before the interviewers could do their work:

K. Buller: Are you trying to identify both the positives and the barriers? Is that what you're trying to do, without really touching too much on the negative?
K. Banks: Yeah, if you can see the barrier and you don't want it ...
K. Buller: The barrier is a negative, then.
K. Banks: ... you can maybe dismantle it. If you don't want it there, and a whole bunch of other people don't want it there, you can dismantle it. If everybody individually comes up against it and says, 'Oh, I'll just dodge around it this time' ...
John: Like the co-operative apartments, all the neighbours got together. They didn't want that tree torn down, they didn't want it cut down. It was right in the middle of the road. They stood up, and it's still there.
Gail: What you're saying is, barriers are not necessarily a negative.
Wayne: I think that a good neighbour is somebody who stays at home, and Ken (Buller) thinks that it is one who comes out and does his part.

K. Buller: Well, give me a barrier that's a good thing, then.

Wayne: You're saying that 'barrier' and 'negative' are the same thing, and I'm saying not necessarily.

K. Buller: It's not up to us to define what is right or wrong, but it is possible for us to define positive and negative.

Gail: Well, no. You can identify people's feelings, negative feelings, but it doesn't mean that ...

Wayne: It's right or wrong.

Gail: Yeah. And what we want to find out are, what are the general strengthening factors in neighbourhoods and neighbouring relationships, and what are the weakening ones?

It was sometimes surprising to all of us to learn that simple, everyday words were so contentious. We eventually found consensus on a locally acceptable meaning for the word 'barriers,' but only after spending half of one meeting on that one term. Words such as 'intimacy' proved more problematic. Most of the interviewers saw 'intimacy' as clearly a sexually loaded term and could not comfortably use it in a larger context. The academic members of the team saw it as relating to closeness in many kinds of relationships, while the local members saw it as having highly sexual connotations. Gail and Ken had even thought of making 'intimacy' one of the central themes, alongside concepts such as 'privacy,' 'belonging,' and 'self-image.' After much debate, however, we replaced 'intimacy' with another, more neutral term: 'association.'

In approaching these discussions, we did not wish to be seen as imposing our form of discourse, nor did we want to be dismissive or demeaning to counter-arguments. We wanted to probe and explore the connotations of local understandings and to use such occasions to begin the process of reflective dialogue with our research participants. The debates went on for months over the significant words, revealing the ways in which they, and the ideas they represented, were important to the people involved. In what follows, we attempt to recount the outcomes of those debates.

Community

Expressing the Meaning

One of the most problematic concepts was also one of the most central: the notion of 'community.' Ken's field notes from the summer of 1993 reflect this: 'The Company of Neighbours has become a form of mediator between the meanings of the larger outside world and local meanings. Once again, we arrive at the point that the capacity to define things locally seems to be a significant factor in building community.'

Our theoretical readings suggested to us that 'community' was a concept expressed as much through symbolic and ritual action as through more explicit forms of discourse (Low 1993). As we examined and re-examined our data, we therefore began to look not so much for a discussion of the meaning of community as for more indirect expressions of the forms and nuances of community. By examining those implicit, often non-verbal expressions first, we set the stage for a comparison with more formal theory.

One of our clearest and earliest findings was that many people in Hespeler had a strong sense of history and that it was the key to understanding many commonly held norms. This notion of community was and is based on particular knowledge of individuals and their shared commitment to historically rooted practices, as well as an awareness of their shared physical and architectural heritage.

Here is one story of a struggle to save a local institution – the Boy Scouts' Hall, built with local volunteer labour in the early part of this century. (In reporting on these interviews, we do not use names as we did with our interviewees. We identify the interviewer only as 'Ixx,' and the respondent as 'Rxx,' in order to protect their confidentiality. To distinguish the voices being reported, we identify different respondents and their interviewers with different suffix numbers.)

I1: They wanted to tear the Scout Hall down too.

R1: Yeah. Oh, I voted against that. My dad and I went to the meeting. My father helped build that Scout Hall, you know, and I spoke up at the meeting. I said, 'You just want to tear it down. Use it! Make use of it. It's a good building, fix it up.' I mean, people put a lot of hard work into that. And like I said to them, my dad was proud to say he helped build that Scout Hall. And he put a lot of hours in there, along with a lot of other people from this town. And there's no way they should have torn that down. And they didn't. They listened to us for a change.

I1: It looks pretty good, too.

R1: Yeah it does. They've done a nice job of it. My dad, the guy was working down there, and Dad was walking by, when he was walking in the park. He said to him, you know, he had helped build it, when it was first built. He [the worker] said 'come on in, I'll show you what we've been doing.' And he was really amazed at what a nice job they'd done to it.

The old Scout Hall and the old arena were both built by local residents. The arena was demolished by the city of Cambridge in 1988, to the dismay of many residents, who did not believe that it was unsafe. Even its replacement with a modern new building has not healed the wound. An ironic portrait of the original arena, which was styled like a Swiss chalet, now hangs in the corridors of the sanitary new structure, with a brass plaque saying 'We Will Not Forget.' The Scout Hall and, more recently, the historic Black Bridge on the edge of town are a different story. Both were saved and restored as local people drew on their sense of historical community and learned to play the political game within the new social and organizational context.

For us, these events raised several new questions about the embodied definition of community. Are communities that were formed around municipal boundaries still defined by the municipality when the borders change? Are buildings more than public utilities? Are blood, sweat, and tears more powerful in the maintenance of community than documents that give authority to demolish or build? Some of the answers would come in later phases of the project (see chapter 5).

Problems and Solutions

When we were first constructing our interviews to draw out the Hespeler view of community, we, the social workers and novice community recruits, concentrated on the problems in the town. When asked how they would improve Hespeler, respondents frequently enumerated the problems they perceived the community to have. They often combined these criticisms with expressions of helplessness, frustration, or not knowing what to do.

R2: I don't know. I would make people more friendly to their neighbours, because I think people are too cold here. I would change the way some people react and interact with each other. It's really cold and I just find that sickening. Everybody is so afraid of everybody else that nothing ever gets done about it.

R3: People are too busy going their own way. They don't have time for anybody else. Not even a neighbour.

R4: People are too close together and they can't get along because of their closeness. I don't know how to explain it. I guess they're not busy enough. They're too busy interfering with everybody else's business.

R5: Who knows how to fix it? If someone knew, it would be fixed, right? No one knows the right answers. All they can do is keep cutting back on this and that, but all that's doing is harming the people.

These ruminations constitute a description of what prevents community from happening. Speakers characterized neighbours as too cold, too close together, too busy, or too nosy. The contradictions of multiple perspectives are all too apparent.

Aside from the generalized complaints, many respondents did emphasize on components of the community that might be improved, such as social services, working conditions, and future security:

R6: As far as community services, I don't know. I guess if you look at it, say mental health or counselling services, they need a lot more, in Cambridge.

R7: Machinery has taken over for what people do, so that's one of the reasons there's not going to be that many jobs, because machinery will do it.

R8: By the time we retire there's not going to be a Canada pension for people our age. There will be no money for us because, it's just not going to be there. So we've got to think of it now, and there's so many people out there that don't know that. They don't know that they're not going to be taken care of once they retire. And we try and think of it now, while we're in our late 20s.

Not surprisingly, as people contemplated the economic conditions of the time, they frequently expressed concern about the recession and unemployment. In general, respondents seemed to believe that legitimate cases of hardship deserved support, but most felt that government efficiency, not human need, was the priority in these hard times.

R9: My way of thinking is to cut out some of our social programs and put it into more productive situations. A lot of people are abusing the system. The way we're doing it now, we're just giving them no reason to think for themselves.

R10: I think too many people are taking advantage of it [welfare]. You have to help people to get jobs out there. A lot of people just sit back and take advantage of it. They need more counselling about what's out there, show them that there are jobs that they can do.

R11: I'm saying, if they don't get a job, cut them off. There's lots of jobs. That's what I'm saying. They should take the jobs they have, and if they don't have enough money, give them support on top of that.

In terms of more specifically local problems, one theme that emerged repeatedly was that of concern for teenagers. This was perhaps one of the strongest contrasts with the image of the community in the past.

R12: Get the kids off the street. I think they should have a law. They should have curfew. I don't think it should be ridiculous like 9:00, but 3:00 in the morning is a bit much.

R13: The older kids need skate parks, for instance, areas where they can go and play. There are lots of playgrounds for the children, but there is nothing for the youth.

R14: They had no supervision in growing up for one thing, and they could care less about other people's property. They need a community centre or whatever it's called, where they can go and do things so they won't be causing trouble.

One of the other obvious changes in Hespeler over the last few decades has been the decline of the central shopping district. The resulting inconvenience was frequently commented on, as well as the deleterious effect on casual neighbourly encounters. For some people, the solution was to try to revitalize the feeling of a village centre. Others saw a need for more modern shopping facilities.

R15: You want something that's close and that's convenient and ... they miss having that convenience of going downtown, getting what they need and walking home, especially in the summertime. And we need our post office back.

R16: A drug store would be good for downtown. Either a grocery store or a small variety store, general store or something.

R17: I would like to see a really up-to-date restaurant downtown. A really nice restaurant. I think there's too many of these craft stores. I know what store I'd love to see in downtown Hespeler, a clothing store. And another store I liked was that little nick-knack store, the five and dime. You could go in there and pick up anything.

R18: I would like to see, like I said, the downtown of Hespeler brought back to life, like an Elora or a St Jacob's type of place, or Elmira, you know? Just very home-feeling. And same with the people that live in it.

Clearly, there was an acute awareness among some respondents of the problems within the community. More commonly, however, people demonstrated not just awareness of problems but also recognition of strengths within the community and offered constructive suggestions for change. Several respondents indicated that they would be willing to get personally involved in projects to improve Hespeler:

R19: We have the arena, we have the swimming pool, we have Zehr's plaza, hairdressing, your banks and everything around here. I don't know, I really quite like it here.

R20: I would like to see more help for the older people. I would like to volunteer for the seniors. Taking them out to go shopping or taking them for trips.

R21: I would want more volunteer workers here and people who can afford to give more. You also need more volunteer workers in the disease foundations like kidney, liver, and heart. I'm doing that right now.

R22: I think, first of all, I'd make a place that's easier for kids to go to, to get help, because too many kids have problems with their parents and they don't have anywhere to go. And when they do go, a lot of places just tell them to go on welfare and leave home. Just work it out on your own, and that's not the way it should be. It should be a family unity, and you should all work it out together.

Thus participants indicated a sense of their heritage, awareness of the shortcomings of their community, and willingness to work towards various forms of improvement. They told us of their sense of loss, but also of their efforts to save the remnants of their past. The interviews gave us insights into Hespelerites' conception of their community, through both their identification of central institutions and their descriptions of the social relationships that constitute and define that community. In pondering these expressed meanings, we were led to reconsider classic theories of community relations and their meaning for the larger society.

Theoretical Conceptions

One of the most compelling images defining the relationship between society and community comes from Max Scheler, the brilliant, unconventional German sociologist. Scheler was developing his theories as Hitler's National Socialists were consolidating their hold on German society in the 1930s: '"Society" is not the inclusive concept, designating all the "communities" which are united by blood, tradition and history. On the contrary, it is only the *remnant, the rubbish* left by the inner *decomposition* of communities. Whenever the unity of communal life can no longer prevail, whenever it becomes unable to assimilate the individuals and develop them into its living organs, we get a "society" – a unity based on mere contractual agreement' (Scheler 1961, 166).

In conceptualizing community as it related to the Company of Neighbours, we found this perspective essential. Our respondents told us repeatedly of the submersion of their community in a larger, more impersonal society. We heard how people interacting in local communities constantly shift and change the particulars of their relations and therefore constantly refresh and enliven the underlying unity of community life.

By contrast, when neighbours' welfare is left completely up to the policy-driven, contractual relations of the state, we witness the decomposition of community. The bureaucratic welfare state may be more formally egalitarian, it may be more efficient, but regulatory and contractual responses to the welfare needs of people are invariably impersonal and ultimately alienating. These 'mere' contractual relations cannot replace the intimate, detailed, ongoing relations that confirm people as part of the 'living organs' of their community.

A similar theme was developed by Anthony Cohen, drawing on the work of Georg Simmel. He observed: 'The anatomy of social life at the micro level is more intricate ... than among the grosser superstructure of the macro-level' (Cohen 1986, 32–3). Humans must and will associate with each other, with or without rules and procedures. As Cohen argues, 'A community may lack formal structures of leadership. However, it will have means of attributing status and prestige' (33). The structures that define a genuine community emerge spontaneously. Formal organization is an overlay that can inhibit these spontaneous structures instead of promoting them.

Other theorists have said that genuine community is made up of those relations that link individuals to one another in social action. Such relations may or may not draw their context from a geographical sense of place. There is a need for face-to-face interaction, but the locus does not by itself define the communality. Emile Durkheim (1957) posited the existence of a 'moral community.' He considered it a concept that transcends individuals – it can both coerce them and command their loyalty and respect. For Durkheim, the moral individual gains his or her dignity from earning trust and developing a shared commitment to commonly held norms, so that aspects of individual self-interest are harmonized within the moral community.

Thus, though Hespeler residents might not articulate their sense of community in the same terms as trained sociologists, their lived sense of their community fits fairly well with some of the classical sociological models. Their interview responses resonated with a sense of 'blood, tradition, and history' and conveyed regret at the passing of some of the micro-structures that had held historic Hespeler together. The problems that they identified often involved violations of local norms and the shared sense of moral community.

Social Rituals and the 'Hardly Worth Mentioning'

Modern society has thrived on superstructure and hierarchy over the last several centuries, and these structures have had a considerable impact on daily life. But the intricacies of micro-community have carried on regardless, as they did in the Middle Ages. Most participants in the Company of Neighbours took these ordinary, routine, and often sociable activities for granted as part of the fabric of their everyday routines. In a phrase that we often heard when we inquired about informal social structures, they were 'hardly worth mentioning' by those who took part in them. But for community developers looking for the materials from which to begin the rebuilding of mutuality, these 'hardly worth mentioning' groups and activities have great significance.

For example, people in Hespeler would frequently go out for coffee at the local fast-food joints and donut shops or for a beer and chicken wings at the pubs. Also, as we heard in our interviews, women whose husbands disapproved of them socializing singly in the evenings would organize 'parties,' where Tupperware or lingerie were sold to friends and family. Such informal gatherings are primarily for casual enjoyment, but that does not preclude the sharing of important information or the reinforcement of vital norms and ideas. People may discuss politics, or the most recently rumoured case of domestic violence, or possibly more personal accounts of family problems or under-employment. When we discussed 'social networks' with our participants, they rarely mentioned such casual events; if pressed, they would indicate that they were 'hardly worth mentioning.' To our sociological eyes, however, they were occasions for the maintenance and reproduction of the informal social structures that sustained the community.

Stories of such gatherings indicated to us the centrality of casual encounters and celebratory social events in the construction and maintenance of a sense of community (see Scott 1969). Throughout the history of North American settlement, through sewing bees, dances, and barn-raisings, celebrations have functioned both to cement personal relationships and to accomplish necessary practical tasks. As we see below in chapter 5, this insight became central to the action phase of the Company of Neighbours.

The research team gradually fine-tuned the questions for the interviews, in order to draw out stories that would demonstrate how relations that constitute community were socially constructed every day by the people in that community. We began to hear about the ways in which social support networks were maintained and also about community problems that arose from the weaker components of those networks. In what follows, excerpts from our group dialogues and interviews narrate the local definition of key elements of mutuality in the words of Hespeler's people.

Mutual Aid

Our interviews regarding people's support networks were fairly open-ended but drew on a number of central concerns and reflected some basic assumptions. For instance, we suspected that people do have rather tenuous emergency plans in the back of their minds in case of a 'rainy day.' The locally recruited interviewers were able to evoke some insights from their friends and neighbours when they asked if the interviewees had actually put any thought into what they would do if the safety net were cut out from under them:

I23: Let's say your parents got laid off, and things were going to be tougher than they already are.
R23: We'd be living in a cardboard box.
I23: Wouldn't that bother you?
R23: For sure. I'd probably have to move in with my Uncle K.
I23: You seem to get along well with him.
R23: Yeah, but if I moved in with him, he'd probably stop liking me as much. I don't know.
I23: You think that people who live together tend to have clashes?
R23: For sure.
I23: Have you ever had a major fight with your uncle?

R23: No. Once I thought we did, I left the light on in his car, and he started yelling at me, and I started yelling back, and then I went into my house, and a bit later he came in saying, 'Hey, do you want to go out for something to eat?'

This young man believes that he has only his uncle between him and living in the cardboard box in the street. It may be that he has not thoroughly checked out community resources, because the reality of scrambling for shelter is for him still theoretical, but it is on his mind. He believes that he could rely on his family, but he knows that relationships can chafe in close quarters.

Participants were asked who they turned to in times of stress, or in times of celebration. We discovered that when it came to having someone 'there for you,' intimate networks played a critical role. Respondents had clear ideas about the strengths and difficulties of seeking help among close or familiar relationships.

R24: I'm so busy, but I know my friend is there, and she's there anytime I want her, and she understands, because she knows how busy I am. You make the time when you have the time to make, that's the thing about a friend. They'll be there when you need them.

R25: So again I think just good friends is the answer. People that I feel comfortable and that ... and I feel really do care about my situation. There's no sense talking to somebody who may be a friend but you don't feel comfortable.

R26: I'd probably call my friend in Cleveland. I don't know, she's very sarcastic and I kind of like that. In a funny way, and that's what I like.

Listening that was supportive and non-judgmental was cited several times as the most useful response in a crisis.

R27: It's helpful when you can even, just spill your guts to somebody, and have somebody else be aware of a difficult time you're going through.
I27: Just to be there to listen.
R27: Yes, even that is important in itself.

R28: I can't remember how many times we sat in the driveway of my house, or his house, depending who drove, for two, three or four hours, talking. Mostly me talking and him listening, but that's all it takes. I don't know how many times I'd just let out the problems that I was going through.

I29: You mean somebody patient ...

R29: ... to teach me how to do it step by step. Somebody can show me what to do and – bang, I can do it. But somebody has got to be real patient. As soon as I see impatience, if somebody gets treating me like I'm stupid, I lose all my confidence and that's it, it's down the drain and I don't even want to try it again.

Honesty and trust were notable features of these interactions. It was also important to know that the people to whom one turned would 'always be there' for them and that they themselves could be counted on in turn.

R30: Honesty ... just honesty. If something's bothering you, you tell the person.

R31: And she's truthful and she's honest, and if I ask her something, whether it was what I wanted to hear or not, I know that she would tell me the truth.

R32: Because we're always there for one another ...

R33: She is always there when I need her.

I34: So she's been a real support for you, your granddaughter?
R34: Yes, I don't know what I'd do without her, she's my right arm. I'm going to live with her for a while. If I'm there I always help.

Familiarity, a confidant's intimate knowledge of their life, seemed to provide comfort to these respondents, and a sense of belonging. Awareness of mutual history was an important factor when they sought people out in both good times and bad. Their stories depict friendships grounded in sharing a sense of fun, as much as support in rough times.

I35: If you're bursting with joy, what do you do?
R35: Go out. I call my friend downstairs, and usually he's willing to go out, but if he's not, I call my friends from Preston, and if they're not, I call my friends from work. Out of those three, one of them's always willing.

R36: It's not like going into a normal bar where you sit at your table and listen to the band or you get up and dance. That place is like a reunion hall – everybody goes in and talks.
I36: It's like a meeting place.
R36: Yes. It's like going to a stag and doe or something, where everybody knows everybody.

R37: Well, it's always the same guys too. We're like a family. We've known each other for years and we all went through good times and bad times together.

While respondents appreciated and even sought advice, it was clearly secondary to just being heard.

I38: And she'll listen to you?
R38: Oh, yes, we tell each other almost everything. I would feel relieved afterwards.
I38: Does she advise you?
R38: Yes.
I38: Do you listen to the advice?
R38: Sometimes.

Several respondents mentioned that alcohol played a role in social support, for alleviation of stress, but also in times of celebration and socializing. It seems that though alcohol was an important prop, the comfort of association with friends and familiar faces was primary.

I39: What do you do to alleviate the stress you're feeling?
R39: Well, usually no, I don't usually have a beer. Well, sometimes I have a couple, but never many. Usually we all get together and kind of mourn together. And everyone as a group, then, we all take it as a loss.
I39: Does it help?
R39: Oh yeah, for sure. Because you know that there are people that care for you.

I40: If you're lonely, what do you do?
R40: I'm never lonely.
I40: Never in your life?
R40: Well, if I was lonely, I'd usually go out with the boys and party 'er up.

I41: If you're bursting with joy, what do you do?
R41: Crack a beer.

Closeness and familiarity also imply particular difficulties, however. Respondents generally believed that the role of family and friends was one of mutual support. When reaching out to family or friends resulted in unexpected rejection or betrayal, the pain was felt acutely:

I42: Do you confide in your husband's side of the family?

R42: I wouldn't confide in them if I was dying. I didn't push my luck and I didn't ask for anything, because I did ask for one thing once, and I got turned down in a not-so-pleasant manner. And I never asked for help again.

This bit of dialogue reminds us that support is not always available when needed. In addition to expressions of friendship and neighbourly inter-action, many respondents reported feeling isolated, cut off, or alone. Some indicated that they were aware of the financial and emotional burdens already experienced by their families and friends. They spoke of the many pressures of modern life that hinder close relationships.

R43: I don't go to them financially because none of them are in a financial position to help me.
I43: Do you miss having a best friend here?
R43: In a way I do.
I43: What's stopping you from having one?
R43: It's because everybody is busy, that's what's stopping me from having one. You're busy, I'm busy, you don't like to impose.

R44: Family? They all got their own things to do.

I45: You really rely on your family a lot?
R45: Yes, well, who's around to help me? J's had troubles, he lost his wife. The baby's in you-know-what – the cooler.
I45: In jail?
R45: Yes.

I46: Do you have family and friends beyond your immediate clan here in Hespeler?
R46: Just in Mississauga, I have an aunt and uncle and I have a few cousins, but we only see them maybe once a year. We get Christmas cards, from them, but as for socializing, we don't. I've never really known my mother's family or my father's family.

I47: Do you like your neighbours?
R47: Yeah. I don't get to know them that much. They're more sort of Toronto people coming in, bringing in the Toronto atmosphere.
I47: So are you saying you don't associate with them on a regular basis, or you do?
R47: Oh, well, we have the 'Hi' and 'Goodbye.'
I47: Why do you leave it at that?

R47: Well, you don't want to exactly push yourselves on them. Wait for the invitation. When they get around to it. Right now, they're too busy renovating the house.

For some, the sense of isolation was compounded by a feeling that their neighbours could not be trusted with the details of their personal problems:

R48: Well, once they all find out about your problem, they all talk about it, and talk behind your back, and things like that. It's not always good talking. So that's one reason why you don't want to be talking, except to relatives. They don't keep it to themselves. They tell the next one, and, you know, along like that, so ... And it's not something to talk about. But they do anyway.

I49: How do you like your neighbours? Do you know any of them?
R49: I used to know a lot of them, but I've stopped hanging around them. The adult ones are alright, except for the thieves.
I49: So, you don't associate with them on a regular basis. And the reason is?
R49: Well, there aren't really that many kids around, they're all adults, and they're kind of cool, but they're all thieves and stuff.
I49: How do you know they're thieves?
R49: Everybody knows.

In a crisis, however, people hope that someone they know and who has connections to people who care is in the area.

I50: Who helped you?
R50: J.K. come along and he said 'Nanna, what happened, did you fall?' I said, 'Well it looks like it, I'm down here and I can't get up.' Then another guy come down around the corner in his truck, and between them they got me up.
I50: And took you to the hospital?
R50: Well, J. helped me back in my apartment, and I was just going to bathe it with the cold tap and wrap it up, which I would have done, and J. said, 'get on that phone and call [granddaughter] or I'm calling an ambulance, you gotta go to the hospital.'

Not surprisingly, we found a wide range of relationships and attitudes within this community and a variety of expressions of those relationships. Many people did have others on whom they knew they could rely. But for some, Hespeler was a cold place, where friends who could be trusted were few and far between. It is for these people, of course, that traditional social-work institutions were established, and we found that formal counselling agencies provided some support in very specific ways. The value of having a safe place to 'ventilate' was relayed by one respondent. However, professional help was not always viewed as accessible or successful.

R51: I was able to do a lot of yelling, and I felt better for it afterwards, because I was able to say things to him in an environment where I was secure and I was safe, and knew he couldn't do anything to retaliate, whether he liked the answer or not. It was positive in the sense that I felt better. The reason we were going was to help my mother. It didn't do a damn thing, in fact it probably caused more trauma for her than anything.

R52: There's really no one you can turn to if you have a lot of problems.
I52: What about counselling, and that?
R52: There's not much counselling out there, I don't think.
I52: So you just, in other words, you just work it out yourselves.
R52: Yeah.

R53: I'm discouraged from counsellors, totally discouraged from them, so I know for sure I wouldn't go back to counselling. Not unless they could prove to me that they're going to offer more help or something. Say more than 'uh huh, uh huh.' I can do that myself.

One woman chose not to join a therapy group because she felt that she could not trust others to keep her problems in confidence:

R54: I would feel too intimidated, and I'd feel that I'm being laughed at by the rest. I could never go in a group session like that. It would have to be a one-on-one where nobody knows my secrets. I couldn't let a whole bunch of people know. No way.

Respondents expressed greater confidence in advice based on experiential knowledge rather than on professional expertise:

R55: Well, first of all, I don't like people trying to run things when they don't know themselves. You can't learn stuff like that, to me you can't learn that much by books.

R56: You have to experience a lot of things in order to actually say you're qualified. All the learning in the world won't prepare you for what's really out there.

R57: We've got a long-term friendship. She gives me more support because her kids have gone through everything you can imagine. So anything I tell her is not new for her. I can get an indication as to whether I should take something seriously or not.

The transcripts presented above show clearly the range of intimate relationships, and the complex of personal feelings, experienced by participants in our project. They highlight the importance of having someone to listen and the variety of friends, relatives, and neighbours to whom people turn. Social networks begin with these intimate feelings and relationships, and their significance to people's everyday lives is apparent. For a number of reasons those uplifting conditions are not present for many people, and the present social and political climate frequently means that such people are simply out of luck. Unless they can locate their own forms of social support, disadvantaged people will be left behind in the era of 'global competition.' Neo-conservative ideologues seem to believe that welfare can be privatized, if not eliminated (see Ehrenreich 1997) – that government intervention is some sort of interference in the 'natural' processes of social sorting. But theirs is not the only viable image of human nature and human society.

Theoretical Conceptions of Mutuality

In Canada today, a great deal of public policy, and of theorizing in the field of social support, assumes that competition – the struggle for dominance and the relations of the marketplace – are the exclusive factors governing the behaviour of human beings. Darwin's (1989) and Wallace's theories of the survival of the fittest have been applied to human affairs, and have become an almost universal modern dogma that shapes the institutional forms of our society. There is not much room for mutuality – mutual support as an enlightened form of shared self-interest – in a world where every human is pitted against every other in competition over the means of existence. What has been lost as this dogma has taken hold in the twentieth century is the memory that social Darwinism is not the only theory of species being. There is a body of theory, backed by strong evidence, which counters the notion that global competition is a universal 'law of nature.'

Prince Peter Kropotkin, for instance, was a Russian biologist, geographer, and ecologist. His global studies and subsequent theories countered the widely promulgated theories of evolution of Charles Darwin.

Kropotkin published around the same time as Darwin, in the 1880s and 1890s, culminating in a major book entitled *Mutual Aid: A Factor in Evolution* in 1904 (Kropotkin 1989). While Darwin acknowledged the role of mutuality in his early work, social Darwinians largely ignored this aspect of his theories. Kropotkin's meticulously arrayed field data supported an argument for an underlying principle of mutual aid, which he saw as being responsible for the flourishing of all surviving species of animals – particularly humans.

Though Kropotkin was a celebrated scientist of the Victorian era, he was also an anarchist. His theories were discredited for political, as much as scientific, reasons. The modern interests of capital helped to canonize a view of humankind that fostered institutionalized competition. In contrast, Kropotkin argued that there was no evidence that competition for survival drove the success of the species that he studied.

Two aspects of animal life impressed me most during the journeys which I made in my youth in Eastern Siberia and Northern Manchuria. One of them was the extreme severity of the struggle for existence which most species of animals have to carry on against an inclement Nature; the enormous destruction of life which periodically results from natural agencies; and the consequent paucity of life over the vast territory which fell under my observation. And the other was, that even in those few spots where animal life teemed in abundance, I failed to find although I was eagerly looking for it that bitter struggle for the means of existence, *among animals belonging to the same species* which was considered by most Darwinists (though not always by Darwin himself) as the dominant characteristic of the struggle for life, and the main factor of evolution. (Kropotkin 1989, xxxv).

If mutual aid is as much a part of animal nature as is competition, then we may find that it is even greater among humans. Individual humans clearly cannot survive alone – we require a supportive society to live. The question then becomes only the degree to which that supportive society expresses its tendencies towards mutual aid.

As community developers, we were concerned to locate a foundation of community spirit within this context, on which it would be possible to begin the rebuilding of mutuality. Through our interviews, we began to perceive the basic elements of the micro-structures of mutuality. Our response to our initial findings was to address what people were willing to work on, in the name of contributing to a predilection towards community life at the macro level. So, while our overall goal was to address the psychosocial and material effects of the reduction of the social safety net, we found that mutuality in the whole community had to be resuscitated before safety-net issues would even be considered. We came to believe that this approach, while time-consuming, would lead to the longest-lasting results for overall community development. Armed with this insight, we began to look at how people related to the larger social structures of their community.

Local Organizing of Basic Social Tasks

Our interviews quickly confirmed that the family is the most basic institution that is used to organize social supports. Though most of us take its workings for granted, we often perform familiar tasks strategically and with careful communication, as shown by this man talking about his relationship with his grown children:

R58: There is a line that you have to travel, that doesn't step into their life so much that it interferes. But there's still the belonging feeling, the understanding feeling. But you've got to be there, you've got to be careful with how much you step back, even. You can step back too far from them. Once in a while, I see that happening, both in my wife and in myself, and we try to adjust things accordingly, and talk about it.

I58: How long do you think that will continue?

R58: Oh, it will go on as long as they're in this area. I would say that distance could change that to a certain extent. If any of them were moving far afield, and because of jobs, or because of this desire to see new country, you wouldn't be able to stay as current with all the little things that are happening. And, because of that, you would lose the closeness of it all. That doesn't mean that it's going to be detrimental to either yourself, or them.

I58: But there's just not that constant being in touch?

R58: Yeah. I think that with the increase in responsibility and pressure that everybody seems to feel nowadays, it almost tends to help people stay close, because of the increased need to support. Mentally, you know, morally.

I58: You mean, the fact that the bigger you are, the more you need things to hold you together?

R58: The older you get, we used to say, well, let's put it this way: there was the empty-nest syndrome feeling, where the kids, you expected them, eighteen, nineteen years old, to head out. But now certainly the extra financial responsibility is keeping kids in the house much longer than they used to be. It appears the only thing that drives kids out of the house nowadays is any abuse they might be suffering.

I58: Well, they're not getting married as early as they used to.

The church draws many people together, each bringing his or her own skills and needs to gatherings:

I59: And you've both always been involved with the church as you were growing up?
R59: Yes.
I59: Have you found that your children have pretty much followed in your footsteps as far as religious instruction goes? I know in my family, as soon as we were old enough to make up our own minds about going to church, half of us stopped going.
R59: That's pretty much the way it is here too. I guess it's just the different generation. But even among my own brothers and sisters, there was a time when some of them didn't go to church, but they came back later on.
I59: When? When they started having children?
R59: Yes. Some of them. Even at that time they didn't all come back. It was an effort. For me, it helps to belong to the choir. That's a good incentive to go, because I feel an obligation to be there. The other people are there to support you. We are a support to each other.
I59: So it's a support system for you?
R59: Really, it is. A social support.

Workplaces are not necessarily organized for social support, but it can become available there too.

I60: Who can you count on to talk about problems related to your workplace?
R60: Well, I think my co-workers.
I60: You would want to relate the problem at all, or not?
R60: Oh, well, there was a small problem to do with a shift. And in my situation, I have a son who is on probation due to a charge that he was charged with and convicted of, and he is on probation and has a ten o'clock curfew. And in my position, we work days strictly, but we have somebody who works nights, and he of course has holidays once a year. My boss decided that I would have to work that shift, and knowing full well of the situation. I wasn't real pleased about that. To make a long story short, I stood up for myself, basically saying I couldn't do it, and left work in a bit of a dither to say the least, without any harsh words spoken. My choice was to leave before it got to that point. And he phoned me from work after I got home, and said he had resolved the situation with another employee, who at the time he said it wouldn't suit, but I had full reason to believe that he never asked him in the first place.

I60: Never even spoke to him?

R60: No. So in any event, I stood up for myself, and he said this person would work it for me. But I phoned after that conversation was over, I phoned my co-worker at home and talked to him about the situation. And it helped. It got some of the pressure off my chest, because it was building up.

I60: It was somebody that you are working with every single day?

R60: Yes, that's right. We spend about eight and a half to nine hours a day, five days a week, and we know each other well. We're counter mates. We both work on the front counter and we know each other real well. We know each other's problems, and talk about each other's problems, even at work when things are slow. Out of the ear shot of other people.

Informal organizations help maintain social supports, too.

I61: Your coffee group must be a real support for the women who belong.

R61: Oh sure. During times of crisis. Definitely. I think that is very valuable, because you're all in the same kind of 'group.' It is really terrific, that coffee group. And still ... Just last week one of the women had her fortieth wedding anniversary, and we were all there. Deaths, anniversaries, whatever, we're together.

I61: The support you've developed for yourself over the years is wonderful.

R61: Yes. But I think it really started for most of us once we started having children ... when you 'settle down,' that's when you start building the support for yourself.

Families, churches, workplaces, and informal gatherings – these are the social 'remnants' of genuine community. Reflecting on the roles of these institutions, and the ways they were used for social support, led us to consider how they might be energized and brought together for new forms of social action. It was in this regard that we found the traditions of activist community education, from Canada and elsewhere, to be most relevant.

Redefinitions

Revisiting Theories of Community Education and Action-Research

Traditions of activist community education in Canada go back at least as far as the Great Depression. Father Moses Coady worked in the Antigonish region of Nova Scotia in the 1930s and later. He believed in cooperative organization through an educated populace: 'We can, in co-operation with other people and educational institutions, give to the rank and file of the people of the world what might be called a liberal education and thus prepare them for economic, social and cultural development down the long reaches of the centuries ahead' (quoted in Laidlaw 1971, 91–2). Following Coady's lead, church workers and local educators used the support of the Extension Department of Saint Francis Xavier University to develop study groups throughout the region (Armstrong 1977). In the study groups, stories would be told of 'what common people had done in other parts of the world' (Laidlaw 1971, 81–92). Over time, cooperatives were formed to serve the needs of local farmers and merchants. These institutions had a powerful influence over the local economy, providing stability when other areas of the province were in desperate straits. Coady's followers believed that mutuality among people was a world-wide phenomenon, which could become the basis for a new form of social organization.

These ideas were developed under the rubric of 'Popular Education and Conscientization' by Paulo Freire and his associates, starting in the late 1950s in northern Brazil (see Freire 1973; Freire and Macedo 1987). Freire developed a thorough-going critique of modern education and a set of radical alternative practices. Like Coady, Freire worked with poorly educated people in a search for knowledge, and a critical reflection on reality, followed by action that allowed them to transform conditions for their whole community (Campfens 1997, 37).

Back in Canada, social workers in Quebec were influenced by church workers who returned from 'conscientization' work in Brazil. Self-administration projects and cooperatives developed during this time, as part of what would later be called 'community economic development' (Alary 1990). As in Nova Scotia, cooperatives made up of participants who were also owners and users, producing products and services for members at cost, became a great strength to many communities in Quebec and elsewhere. Doré (1997) describes how women in low-income areas worked with community workers to articulate their needs and to get at solutions.

Over the last several decades, there has been a strong movement in Quebec, grounded in the parish system that was the foundation for earlier forms of social organization related to the Catholic church. Alary and his colleagues fostered a fundamentally different way to deliver social and health services, based on a concept of solidarity known as 'social animation.' This idea is akin to mutuality, as it views the behaviour of humankind as grounded in dual recognition of both individual differences and common desires (Alary 1990, 11).

These ideas have taken hold in Saskatchewan and are deeply rooted in Native communities throughout Canada. But given the political ideology of Ontario today, the idea that human behaviour is grounded in anything other than competition seems to be heresy there. Perhaps we could add another quarter-century to Braverman's (1974) observation: 'The idea that we are somehow self-integrated units that can be transferred anywhere, plugged into the system, repaired when we break down, or warehoused when not needed by the workforce, has become increasingly dominant in the last fifty years' (87). Our data suggest that many people today are caught up in a contradictory ideology typical of modern life. They pay lip-service to conventional wisdom about global competition but continue to organize among themselves the mutuality that they need to survive.

Toward a Redefinition of Community and Mutual Aid

The contrast between the research team's initial approach to defining community and that of community members has come into bold relief in this chapter. We began by encouraging our local interviewers to draw out problems in the community, only to have our friends, the interviewers, challenge us on the meaning that we attributed to key concepts. When we asked local residents to conceptualize community by identifying Hespeler's problems, they were frequently frustrated and expressed their sense of powerlessness over their lives. However, when we shifted our approach to that of drawing out the strengths and weaknesses of their personal lives in the community, they spoke with a depth of knowledge and confidence that was not evident before. Micro-community life and family life were what the interviewers, our community partners, said that we should be looking into – these were the elements that outside researchers called 'networks.' If we asked Hespelerites what worked and what did not work in organizing the events of their lives, they were able to tell us about talks with friends, huddles with spouses, and the strength of spirit among the old and vulnerable – the necessary but 'hardly worth mentioning' relations that make up communal life.

Thus the tensions between our theoretical readings and our dialogues with residents led us to an analytic focus on the symbolic and ritualistic manifestations of 'community.' These themes were to shape the Company of Neighbours as the project progressed. One of our central discoveries was that people in Hespeler would happily organize around public events connected to culture or recreation but would not usually intrude in what they perceived to be the private affairs of their friends and neighbours. As a result, our earliest efforts, as we entered the action phase of our project, attempted to revive and promote some 'old-fashioned' community rituals.

Early Outcomes

Even though we had provided for an information-gathering stage at the beginning of the project, there were times in the early days when it seemed that our strategy of not imposing structure and programs was not working very well. Hespelerites frequently challenged us as to what we 'really' wanted to know, and to do, within the community. Our attempts to be non-directive and open seemed to them to be vagueness or evasion.

Gradually, however, people began to drop into the office to chat, especially after we started training the interviewers and conducting interviews. A small group of older residents started to come in on a regular basis to share stories. Eventually, they organized the History Group, which would later become central to the project's activities (see chapter 4). We listened to their stories, but no clear direction or theme was being generated by our activity, after almost six months in the community.

Then, beginning in the summer of 1993, a few locally generated ideas launched a process of community revival that was to snowball over the next three years. Stewart Walker, who supported himself by tutoring French students and managing fourteen newspaper routes, offered to help edit and deliver a community newsletter which became known as the *Beehive*. A city-sponsored refurbishing of the main street was completed, and the Company of Neighbours helped promote reopening of the downtown through a small celebration.

We knew from the interview data that there was great concern for the lack of sanctioned activity for teens in Hespeler. We decided to take some initiative and advertised a program, the 'Evening in the Park,' in the *Beehive*. Every Wednesday evening, three or four of us would go to Forbes Park with musical instruments and baseball equipment. A picnic atmosphere was promoted by the Presbyterian church's having its cookouts on Wednesdays, and we arranged for a local ice-cream store to have special prices on those nights.

We had anywhere from twelve to forty people of all ages come out for the 'Evenings in the Park.' Many who came only to gawk, or to laugh at our amateurish musicianship, were eventually drawn into the fun. John Jeffery and Ken Banks made contact with some of the teenagers who claimed the park as theirs on summer nights. There was some talk of having a coffee house, and a place to perform and listen to music, that teens could operate. We went so far as to call in outside professional consultants who had organized such programs before. But we found that the teens did not want the places offered by the adults, and the adults would not allow the teens into the areas that they preferred, so nothing came of this initiative.

The History Group members had friends at a large local seniors' residence, and they took a display of memorabilia to the institution for their friends to see. Teachers heard of the displays and brought their students to the site office to browse, as a class project. This led to several from the History Group being invited to the schools to talk about local history. At Jacob Hespeler Secondary School, they met the head of the history department, John Jeffery. John became an enthusiastic supporter of the Company of Neighbours that year and began preparing videos of the town and interviews with key storytellers.

That autumn, John invited several members of the History Group to visit his classes. These events were greatly enjoyed by youths and aged alike. We did well with the motivated teens, but the kids on the margins only talked to us and did not follow through on the ideas that we discussed. It was a paradoxical situation, for they seemed to expect us to tell them what to do and how to do it. If we were non-directive, they were suspicious and backed away. But if we tried to lead, they rebelled against such an expression of adult authority.

In the meantime, Joann had taken a computer course and joined the office staff part time. She suggested we address local unemployment directly by setting up résumés for neighbourhood women and flyers for area businesses. We knew that there were a lot of teenaged mothers in town who lacked social support. Joann tried to organize a support group among her friends, but no one showed up. Local agencies and the public health nurse said that they thought it a great idea, but only one of them came to a meeting. We began to recognize the shortcomings of a direct attack on Hespeler's 'social problems.'

While some of our efforts met with frustration, others were great successes. Russell Bygrave, organizer of the locally operated Santa Claus parade, was a regular at our office, and many people enjoyed helping with decorations, raffle-ticket sales, and the packing of candy bags at

Christmas. When Russell later fell ill, volunteers from the Company of Neighbours helped keep the parade alive, until the parade-master could don his white tuxedo once again.

By the time we had completed our first year and a half in Hespeler, we had begun to learn some useful lessons. We had acquired a good deal of insight into Hespeler's social structure. We had tried to remain true to our commitment to an open-ended, participatory, and dialogical process. But when we attempted to articulate and address the problems that had been identified in our interviews, as traditional community workers always have, virtually nothing happened. With more positive celebratory events, however, it was a very different story. The Evenings in the Park, the Santa Claus Parades, and the activities of the History Group showed us that reaffirmations of Hespeler's heritage were the way to revive the community. Such events, and the socializing over coffee or beer that residents considered 'hardly worth mentioning,' were far more effective than the examination of present problems or conjecture about the future.

Gradually, through continuing dialogue with the interviewers' group, the History Group, and the many people whom we met around town, we began to see the emergence of a narrative community. The people of the village got our attention and went about showing us how to accomplish what we had told them was our goal. Our next chapter is about what we learned from them.

4

Retelling and Reclaiming
Hespeler's History

The previous chapter examined many aspects and meanings of community, neighbourly relations, and mutual aid, in terms of their definitions in social theory, their everyday discursive use, and the ways in which they are socially defined through people's actions. In the process of establishing our project in Hespeler, recruiting our local researchers and other participants, and conducting and analysing our interviews, a narrative community started to emerge. We began to get a sense of the residents' beliefs, concerns, and priorities. One of the clearest themes was the great interest in Hespeler's history and concern that the best traditions of the community were on the verge of being lost.

The group of Hespelerites who most clearly came to represent the spirit of the Company of Neighbours was our History Group. Without a great deal of formal structure or bureaucratic leadership, members organized themselves for regular meetings, assembled a considerable collection of historical documents, artefacts, and memorabilia, and eventually instigated the largest single event in Hespeler in the last thirty years: the Great Hespeler Reunion of 1996 (see chapter 5, below).

As we learned from the members of the History Group, Hespeler's history is complex and fascinating, and the group made it clear that it wants it to be told. This chapter attempts to relate the community narrative as we have heard it from the old-timers. By drawing on other local documentary sources that they provided, we try to put their story into a more traditional historiographical context, but only in so far as we consider it necessary for outside readers to comprehend their tales. Equally important, this chapter is about the group itself and how its activities inspired other community members to get involved in Hespeler's rebirth.

What follows is a form of the community narrative, assembled from fragments of our many conversations and constructed through our dialogues with the participants in our project. Beginning in August 1993, a group of men and women began to congregate at the office to tell stories of their own lives and to swap tales of Hespeler's history as they had heard it and lived it. This chapter outlines the story that emerged from their recollections and that led us to focus on the town's vital tradition of community reunions, which helped keep alive Hespeler's sense of itself.

Pathways to Hespeler's History

The Nineteenth Century

Readers may find that the tone of the next two chapters changes considerably from what has gone before. That is because the voices of the local participants will be taking over more and more, as the community narrative develops. There are very few academic or statistical sources regarding Hespeler's founding and growth. In some ways, its history can be taken as typical of many of the small and medium-sized industrial cities of southwestern Ontario. Like its sister towns of Preston and Galt, the village that eventually became Hespeler was originally established near the confluence of the Speed and Grand rivers. At this site, fresh water and the energy that could be drawn from its flow were both abundant. Winfield Brewster, who was prominent in the growth of the town and who became one of its chroniclers, wrote fondly of the ancient role of the townsite as a place along the ancient Indian trails: 'Early French historians relate that they travelled well-beaten trails to and along rivers they visited, among which surely was the Grand. Others tell of a main trail from Burlington Bay to the River Thames near Beachville, which crossed the Grand below Brantford and from which other trails ran south ... and to the north' (Brewster 1993, 10).

As a natural hub of transportation and an obvious mill site, the town grew quickly from its settlement by Europeans in the early nineteenth century. Like other small settlements of the day, it was at first dominated by the families that established businesses and homes there. This pattern of dominance by 'prominent' families continued well into subsequent phases of growth, even as the town became more formally organized and urbanized. As the size and diversity of the local industries increased, the pattern of single-family ownership and operation faded. But even the more complex and impersonal forms of capital management that succeeded the family businesses continued to express a paternalistic attitude towards their workers and their town.

One of our prime sources of information on Hespeler's past was Percy Harvey. He was referred to us by several of the older people who made contact with the Company of Neighbours. Percy is an accomplished storyteller and was one of the last mayors of Hespeler before regionalization. He is also a collector of historical documents and was editor of the 1966 *Reunion Book* (Harvey 1966). At History Group meetings, Percy proceeded to tell about family influences in community building, while other regulars, including Archie Scott, Reg Pryor, and Bill O'Krafka, chimed in with embellishments and laughter.

We had the sense that most of Percy's listeners had heard the stories before, as he was coached to 'tell the one about Jacob Hespeler and the founding of Seagram's Distillery' or 'tell the one about Joseph Bergey and the purchase of the lands from the Natives.' For us, however, and for the younger people who began to attend, the stories were always fresh and enthralling. Percy's encyclopaedic knowledge of the area made a major contribution to our understanding of the town.

As we learned from Percy and his documentary contributions, Abram Clemens was one of the first who had purchased a tract of land in the area, in 1809. While he did not build a home on the site, he did construct the first of several sawmills on the Speed River. Among the earliest colonizing residents of the area were Michael Bergey and his wife, who took up residence in 1828 on a property deeded to her brother, Joseph Oberholtzer of Pennsylvania (see City of Cambridge Archives, 1996). In 1833 Clemens sold his mill to Jacob Hespeler of nearby Preston. He rebuilt it as a stone grist mill in 1847 and later added a distillery and a large woollen mill. By 1859, a railway was being built through the village.

Percy: You see, it started off with Oberholtzer having land, as well as his sons. And Bergey bought some land, right where the post office is now, and he built a cabin, and they called it 'Bergeytown.' And that was 1828. By 1835, Clemens had his mill, and that was the year Jake Hespeler bought Clemens out and moved from Preston down here. And Oberholtzer didn't like the idea of having a town named after his son-in-law, so he changed the name to New Hope. But then Jake Hespeler had a census taken in 1859. And all the railroad people were in town, all the engineers, and there were sufficient numbers of people to qualify it as a village. So it was incorporated as a village, in 1859, under the name of 'Hespeler.' And Jake Hespeler was the first reeve.

Percy seems to know his history pretty well. With a couple of exceptions, his account correlates closely with material published in 1900 by the local newspaper:

In 1849 Hespeler built a distillery in addition to his flour mill, and began the work which has ever since stood as a monument to his energy and enterprise. He cleared the forests, drained the swamps, built roads, and spent many thousands of dollars in necessary and lasting improvements. In 1850, Adam Shaw built a saw mill on the site of the old carriage works building, which same building was built a few years later by the late Robert Forbes, who rented it to Jonathan Schofield to be used as a woollen mill.

In 1858, the Great Western railway was extended from Galt to Guelph, and Mr. Hespeler took advantage of the presence of the navvies to have a census taken, with the result that New Hope, or rather Hespeler, was incorporated as a village on July 12 of that year. The first Village Council being, Jacob Hespeler, reeve, and councillors Adam Shaw, Conrad Nohrgaung, Davis Rife and Chas. Karch. ('Hespeler's Founders' 1900, 3)

Percy knew that it was the interaction of exceptional individuals, such as Bergey and Hespeler, with emerging technologies such as railways and hydro-electricity, that had built the town:

Percy: In 1880, when Sir Adam Beck founded this Ontario Hydro idea, they came into Hespeler. Forbes was American. Due to the fact that he came here as a boy with his uncle, Jacob Hespeler, he had Hespeler sign on first. Then Kitchener, then Toronto.
Archie: You mean on the company charter, Percy?
Percy: Yeah, on the Hydro Commission. When the guys came up from Toronto, the chief said, 'I want to welcome you folks to Hydro.' And Carl, the local chairman, nearly fell through the floor. But I said, 'You have a lot to learn. Do you know that Hespeler was the first town to sign on with the Ontario Hydro?' He went back to the archives, and found I was right. We had a lot of fun with that.

According to Winfield Brewster, 'Bergey ... was more of a dealer and had in fact the reputation of being game to either buy or sell anything that had two ends on it' (Brewster 1993, 30). Other entrepreneurs followed in Bergey's footsteps, buying and selling Hespeler's resources and shaping its future in the process.

Percy: So, Randall sold out to Schwartz, Robert Schwartz, who didn't know anything about manufacturing, and Schofield, who was the manufacturer. And Forbes and Schofield agreed, they said they'd buy each other out, if they so desired. So when Schofield said he'd buy Forbes out, Forbes said 'I'll buy you out.' He came down from Guelph with a cigar-box full of cash on his knee, to pay off Schofield. Schofield had the factory that was up here in Hespeler. But Randall went up to get William Hespeler, and they started a brewery.

Then, Hespeler had to go back to Germany on business. And so he looked up his nephew, Joe Seagram, whose mother was a Hespelerite, to look after his interests. Joe had kind of a keen eye, and he looked the business over, and when he came back he bought his uncle out, and then he bought out the other two guys, and that's the beginning of Joseph Seagram's.

Seagram's Distillers became a corporate giant that was bought out by the Bronfmans, who now own Dupont chemicals and other huge multi-nationals. Ontario Hydro developed into a massive crown corporation, with a mandate to keep reliable electricity available at a reasonable cost to a burgeoning Ontario economy. These are prime examples of the efficiencies that have been sought by the consolidation of many sources into an integrated grid. In the nineteenth century, however, such efficiencies came about not necessarily through rational urban planning. The handshake deals among old-fashioned entrepreneurs, the Seagram boy with a 'keen eye' and family roots in Hespeler, and the influence of his cousin, Adam Beck – these forces, grounded in blood lines, were as important as the economics involved.

Industry Arrives

Also emerging were the large textile mills, which flourished under the ownership of the Forbes family. In 1900, a locally printed monograph reported: 'Over 700 people are employed here, in a great variety of work ... Families containing a number of young people interested in securing employment will find it to their advantage to write this firm ... The ever-increasing business of this company enables it to frequently engage entire families, including all workers from fourteen years of age up, and the steady character of the work makes it a very desirable class of employment for industrious and thrifty families' (*Hespeler, Canada* 1900, 11).

The bustling spirit of the Industrial Revolution fairly crackles out of such promotional literature. Hespeler was never just a one-industry outpost, but neither was it ever to become a huge metropolis. Its population was reported at around 2,500 at the turn of the century (*Hespeler, Canada* 1900, 11), and it had grown only to about 3,500 by mid-century ('Hespeler's 100,000 Friends' 1947). Within such a small town, the influence of a few prominent families, and the tendency for them to form interlocking directorates, was perhaps inevitable: 'When George Alexander, second son of Mr. George D. Forbes, had finished School he too entered the mill to learn the woollen business. In May, 1915, he started in the wool barn and from there – with the exception of 18 months in the air force during the war – went up through the various departments. By 1928 when the mill was sold he had become Vice-President of The Forbes Company and was assisting his father with many of his interests outside the mill, and between times working in the office under D.N. Pannabaker ... He was appointed Director of many Companies: President of Taylor-Forbes and the Kribs Company – now Simplicity Products Limited (Inglis)' (Brewster 1953, 32).

The widespread influence of such 'captains of industry' was considerable, and they assumed civic leadership roles 'naturally':

In the eighty year period 1864–1944, men associated with the textile industry here served as Chief Magistrate a total of 43 years. In the period commencing 1907 when we had both a Mayor and a Reeve due to our increase in population 19 years were spent by textile men as Reeve which included membership in the County Council.

In that same eighty year period men associated with the industry served as Councillor a total of 94 years, so that, during the period, we have a total of 156 years of Municipal service, and if we include Jacob Hespeler who was Reeve, 1859–62 inclusive, and his son, Colonel George, and three gentlemen who were councillors who after 1863 were engaged in Hespeler's mill, the total rises to 164 years.

In that same eighty year period men associated with the textile industry served as members of the Hespeler Public School Board for 110 years, and as Chairman of the Board a further 30 years – a total of 140 years. This in addition to the many years spent on commissions and the like.

So it cannot be maintained that textile men in Hespeler have been remiss in their duties to the public. (Brewster 1993, 45)

What is striking about such stories is that they are so clearly about 'blood, tradition, and history' – the key characteristics of community identified by Scheler many years ago (see chapter 2). These fundamental principles of community life may not be entirely consistent with the more universal values promoted today within our officially multicultural society. But the community narrative of Hespeler clearly reveals their role in its formation and growth. When the patriarch of the textile empire died, Winfield Brewster's (1934, 2) eulogy revealed the many ways in which he had dominated the town's affairs:

THE CHIEF IS DEAD

Today at noon George Forbes passed on.
His going casts a pall over the whole Community.
The whole Town mourns.

For two generations head of our greatest industry.
Thirteen years Mayor.
Gentleman, Sportsman, Good neighbour.
Sponsor of everything clean.
Always trying to help.

Director of Fifty Companies.
Loved by all who knew him.
His word as good as his bond.
Business man of the old school.
Presbyterian. Conservative. Mason.

Such versions of Hespeler's story are, of course, written by the elites about the elites and are clearly self-serving. Even so, they reflect a sense of personal commitment to the building of social institutions, alongside profitable industries, which has largely disappeared in today's corporate society. The Hespeler of old felt that it had a destiny, grounded in the stories of the successful families that built themselves up as examples of personal and corporate virtue and success. To some extent that destiny was fulfilled, as Hespeler became a textile centre and a contributor to Canada's war efforts. Yet, as we see below, Hespeler's heyday was surprisingly short.

Hespeler's woollen mill closed in 1887 and, after changing hands several times, was sold to a large corporation that reopened it and operated it in 1901–2. When the new management suddenly closed it again, one-third of the town's population moved elsewhere. There were hard feelings about this corporate closure, and the vacant mill became known as the 'white elephant.' In 1913 the mill was converted to steelware manufacture and reopened again as Stamped and Enamelled Ware Ltd, employing 250 people at the peak of their operations ('Hespeler Urban Renewal Study' 1967, 9–10).

The kinds of changes that Hespeler began to experience around 1900 were the first inklings of a new style of corporate culture. Ownership of local industries, and the nature of the products that they produced, began to change more frequently. Stock companies with boards of directors took over from family-owned businesses. Yet this new form of capital management retained a paternalistic attitude towards the workers and their town. One of the most common artefacts that we saw in the Company of Neighbours was the corporate photograph, similar to a school-class photo, depicting an entire workforce arrayed as a single group, usually in front of its plant. These symbols, and the traditions of company picnics, sports teams, and other such social events, stretched back to the last century and carried on well past the Second World War (see Bouchier and Anstead 1994).

Institutional Change

The generations following the First World War saw a sea change in the traditional family-based values that built Hespeler, and their associated power structures – a shift that has been examined in some detail in the socio-historical literature (see Corrigan and Sayer 1985; Curtis 1988, 1992). Parallelling the changes in private ownership and management was a restructuring of public institutions. School boards and municipal governments, with their elected boards and appointed committees, started to assume more responsibility for the town's development, in what was supposed to be a more rational, egalitarian, planned way. But there was plenty of personal influence, and even force, applied to help the changes along, as we discovered.

The moral task of shaping children's behaviour, for instance, was no longer totally relegated to family preference. Instead, the preferred standards were enforced at the discretion of the school boards and their teachers (see Houston and Prentice 1988). Archie Scott felt the sting of that enforcement:

Archie: Big Bob Chester and I were on the terraces, making snowballs. And Bob, he sort of jimmied them around the corner. And K. [a teacher] always used to walk out at recess-time with his fedora on, you know, and his stick – he always had his stick with him. So he comes around the corner, and Bob knocks his fedora right off his head. And we were the only two on the terrace. And you weren't supposed to be on the terrace at any time. So we went down to the office, and, oh, he laid it on us. I couldn't even write, you know, because there was a welt up to here, and it was just black and blue.

I go home to dinner, and I was just sitting at the table, trying to cut, and my mother says, 'What's wrong with you?,' and I say, 'Nothing,' and she says, 'Yeah, there is, what's wrong with you?' 'Well, I got a licking.' And my dad was sitting there, and he says, 'What did you get that for?,' and I told him, and he says, 'You were wrong?' and I say, 'Yeah.' So he got up, and he phoned old K., and he says, 'You gave my son a licking this morning.' 'Yeah.' 'What was it for?' 'For being at the wrong place at the wrong time.' 'Well,' my father says, 'You can give my son a licking any time that he does wrong, but if you ever leave marks like that on him again, I'll come up there and break every bone in your body.' And when I went back to school, Old K. came over, and apologized. But he still hit kids after that. He just loved to give lickings.

Percy: And the principal would stand there and cry while the teacher was giving you a licking. K. would do it right in front of the principal, and he would stand there and cry. He was a soft-hearted guy.

Archie: Great guy.

This story reveals the blurring of boundaries between personal and official authority that characterized the transitional period. As the trend towards centralization continued, families had less and less to say about what was taught or what discipline was appropriate, except through their member on the school board. From 1878 on, the curriculum came from the provincial Department of Education (see Prentice 1977).

Schooling was not the only area of local life that was being shaped by the newly centralized, bureaucratized institutions. In terms of day-to-day governance, the locally elected municipal council gradually took over responsibility for maintaining public order. The transition from the informality of the old system to control by municipal agencies such as the police was not always smooth.

Archie: The hotel down here was in quite a mess for a while, you could just open the front door and see right into one of the washrooms. Bill [the mayor at that time] wanted them to clean it up, so he went down and talked to them, but they didn't do anything about it. He warned them that he would be back. So then, at one of the council meetings, he said he wanted somebody to volunteer to come down to the hotel with him after the meeting, and give them the last warning. Nobody would volunteer, so I stuck my hand up, and we went down to the bar.

The guys were sitting around the table drinking, and Bill walked up to the owner, and he said: 'You have one week to get things started here, and if you don't, I'll close you down.' And one of the patrons got up and said, 'You and who else?' and Bill said, 'My council. We'll close you down. That's the last warning.' And he turned to walk out, but one of the guys stuck out his foot, so Bill went down. The fellow says, 'That'll be a warning to you, to watch out if you come back here.' He says, 'Come on outside and I'll show you.' And Bill says, 'I don't fight, but if you're going to force this thing, that's fine with me.' He didn't realize, the fellow, that Bill could really go at it with his dukes, you see. So Bill just took off his coat and went in behind the hotel. And the guy's brother was there, too; and Bill just, well, two smacks and bingo, the guy was out cold.

Rough justice, but the hotel was forced to meet the new standards of an industrializing and urbanizing society. Soon there were municipal by-law enforcement officers and public-health inspectors performing such functions, with the force of law to back them up.

The World Wars

As these changes in social organization were going on, prosperity was returning to Hespeler as a result of Canada's involvement in the Great War. By 1916 the town was a centre of textile manufacture, distilling, furniture assembly, and appliance-making. Demand for its khaki and service-cloth products was high, as it was for its cookware and other goods. Many young men went off to war, creating new opportunities at home. At the height of the First World War, 1,600 people were working in the woollen mills (Hespeler Board of Trade 1916).

The staple nature of the goods produced by local industries allowed them to weather some of the economic downturns between the wars. During the Depression, the paternalism of local textile corporations extended to policies of trying to make sure that every family had at least one breadwinner on the job. Not all labour relations were peaceful, however. As economic conditions generally worsened, unions attempted to organize plants all over Canada, and managers fought them off with every tool at their disposal.

Several of the History Group members recalled a bitterly fought strike at Dominion Worsteds and Woollens (DW&W) in the winter of 1933–4. The Ontario Provincial Police (still referred to by old-timers as the 'goon squad') were called in to control the workers. Their union did not succeed in replacing the factory-organized 'works council' until 1943 ('Union Notes' 1943). The American Standard plant, the 'Stamp,' went out on strike for two weeks over a union-certification vote in 1937. According to the memories of those who participated, or whose parents were involved in the strikes, not much was gained in improved conditions and wages, and management continued to express pride in the way in which it took care of 'their people.'

Domestic labour disputes were interrupted by the outbreak of the

Second World War, during which Hespeler sent 452 people overseas, primarily men. These workers had to be replaced in the mills, as in industries all over the country (McLaughlin 1973, 12). In 1942 the Canadian government established the National Selective Service (NSS). The NSS set out to register all women aged twenty to twenty-four, regardless of marital status, in order to determine how many single females or married women without children could be recruited and moved from the country to industrial areas.

During the war, Dominion Worsteds and Woollens estimated that it recruited roughly 600 people per year for a plant that employed a total of 1,000, indicating major employee turnover. Many women were recruited from Newfoundland, even though it was not part of Canada at the time. Recruited women were loaned the cost of travel to Hespeler by the company, required to take medical exams, and given quarters in company-supervised housing (McLaughlin 1973, 14). Many returned home within the first year, but many more stayed and made a life in 'Upper Canada' (see Spring 1986). Specialized staff of the corporations, and municipally sanctioned 'beneficent' business people, chaperoned these single women and looked after the welfare of working people in the town (McLaughlin 1973, 14).

As the men (and some of the women) of the town went off to the Second World War, DW&W began a newsletter, the *DWW News*, which reported not only on happenings at the plant but also on the activities and fates of former workers who were overseas. Fifty years later, complete sets of reprints of this paper became one of the most popular fundraising items for the Company of Neighbours.

By the end of the war, Hespeler's community leadership had expanded outward from the mills to a more diverse group of local businessmen, who also had the support of the town council. The tasks of community development shifted gradually into the hands of public officials, until by the 1950s they had become a regulated function of the municipality. Through private–public partnerships such as a tourist bureau and a chamber of commerce, economic stimulation became a function of the same local municipalities that cleaned up the streets, sanitized the bars, and organized the populace. The powerful families for the most part retreated to their estates, from which they exercised a less obvious, if no less influential, role.

Modernity Comes to Hespeler

With the coming of a new economic context following 1945, things began to change rapidly in Hespeler. As the economy of the area diversified, Hespeler's traditional industries were once again hit by a major shift in industrial organization, this time known as 'global competition.' A series of mergers, acquisitions, and shut-downs began to erode the town's industrial core and to dissipate its working population. The total workforce of Hespeler, which had been as high as 2,400 during the First World War, was down to 1,900 by 1950, with 1,357 working at the largest employer, Dominion Textiles (as DW&W was now known: see Quantrell 1987, 65–6). By 1955, following the Korean War, the company's labour force had fallen to 552. When it finally closed its doors for good in 1958, many residents were concerned for the town's future.

Diversification of industry was a counter-force to the decline of traditional manufacturing, however, and new jobs returned the workforce to about 2,000 by 1966, in a town whose total population was about 5,000. As Percy Harvey pointed out in an interview, two factors saved local workers from suffering from the closures and diversification of the 1960s. First, many were getting older, and government pension plans were being introduced about the time that the closures started. Second, a new industrial park opened in the northern edge of Waterloo Township, adjoining the southern edge of Hespeler. Thus Hespelerites were not thrown onto the unemployment rolls but were dissipated from the large downtown industries into dozens of smaller concerns, spread throughout the region.

Thus bureaucratic efficiency slowly took precedence over the sense of Hespeler as an 'extended family.' In 1969, the post office began home delivery, which obviated people's need to go downtown every day. The local merchants along Queen Street began to close soon thereafter, particularly when a mall opened a mile from downtown, with ample parking and discount prices. At Queen's Park, a new form of local government was being discussed. As Hespeler was to discover, municipal governments exist only by the grace of the provincial legislature, and during the 1960s and 1970s it began seeking efficiencies of scale through application of the concept of 'regional municipalities.' Unfortunately, this concept of economic efficiency completely ignored the damage done to local communities by depriving them of their identities, and dismantling the work of generations of local residents.

The towns of Hespeler and Preston, and the city of Galt, were to be amalgamated into a new city, to be called Cambridge, with the old municipalities being dissolved. Policing and social services would go to the new regional government, which involved still more cities and towns for miles around. The local councils fought this regionalization, but to no avail. Archie (who was on the town council) and Percy told us about one of the many skirmishes in this battle: the fight over 'equalized assessment,' a way of increasing taxation by realigning property assessments across the new amalgamated municipality.

Archie: Amalgamation took over. We were the ones left with the dirty stick. We were well above the amount of money that the town needed, you know. We had $150,000 in reserve, for one thing. But it disappeared like that in amalgamation, you know.
Percy: Here's another thing that comes into play: equalized assessment, they're trying to equalize the thing.
Archie: We had the first equalized assessment. We were the guinea pigs for Ontario.
Percy: I was sitting on a committee on the amalgamation. I was speaking to the provincial Minister at the time. I said, 'You will not have this [amalgamation] brought into effect until all equalized assessment is done [for Hespeler, Preston, and Galt].' [The minister said:] 'Oh, that's exactly right, we will not have that at this time.' The next year, he's out of it, and Darcy McKeough is in, and bingo! We have the thing and everybody's assessed. It would have been our issue to have it separate.

There were no fist-fights this time, but the power of the Hespeler mayor and council was wiped out completely by amalgamation in 1973. A local woman related the reaction of her father, who was on the town council at the time of dissolution:

Dad came home from a council meeting one night and told me and my mom and the other kids, 'The province has dissolved us. We didn't have a say in it in the end.' He was very upset.

For the proud and industrious people of Hespeler, who had long ago adopted a beehive as their town symbol, the submersion of their identity in an impersonal concept of regional municipal efficiency was a terrible blow. In the years that followed, the rapid changes in the area's economic and governmental structure eroded the community's cohesion. The new Cambridge city council encouraged new housing developments in the area. But these brought primarily commuters, people looking for reasonably priced housing, who tended to shop in the malls and to depend on government agencies to provide the necessary community services. As newcomers, many lacked the interest, or the time, to get involved. Family ties began to have less influence in Hespeler's new suburban destiny. Tradition began to seem archaic, and not particularly useful. The history of Hespeler came to be represented by a few documents in the Cambridge archives and the burnt-out hulk of the old mill.

Today, Hespeler is haunted by the ghosts of its former glories, including the looming presence of several largely vacant factories. To some extent, it is making the difficult transition into the 'information age,' but not as an official municipal entity. Just as its location on the ancient pathways made it desirable in the last century as a trans-shipment point, its centrality to the modern communication systems of southwestern Ontario has made it attractive to internet providers and telephone services. The northern tip of Cambridge (Hespeler) has access to an unusually high number of telephone exchanges and hence a great reach for free phone calls. Six new companies employing over forty people established high-tech communications services in Hespeler in the early 1990s.

The former town of Hespeler, and its identity as an industrial boomtown, are gone, but the living communities that constitute the Hespeler of today remain and offer opportunities for local people to build a life together. One sign of Hespeler's pride is that most of the people who live there still call it by its old name. The Boy Scout troop and the Canadian Legion post still carry the name of Hespeler, as do many other local institutions.

We discovered a strong sentiment within Hespeler to avoid becoming merely another suburban sprawl, dominated by doughnut shops and gas stations. In order to construct a story different from that which has befallen so many other communities with histories like Hespeler's, the members of the History Group have worked diligently at informing one another, other townspeople, and students in nearby schools of where Hespeler came from and where it may be going. One of the linchpins of that effort has been the vital memory of Hespeler's town reunions.

Hespeler's Reunions

Throughout the many changes described above, one great tradition was begun and sustained: the 'Old Boys' Reunions.' The first took place in 1906. It is remarkable that a town of only 2,500 people, which was barely fifty years old, would conceive of such an event. But such was the sense of civic pride, and the belief that those who had left Hespeler would want to return, that a massive celebration was organized. The old newspapers and programs brought into our office depict a series of amusements, parades, sporting competitions, band concerts, and dances that must have been quite a highlight of people's summer.

The second reunion occurred twenty years later, in 1926, and was even bigger. A third was planned for 1946, but that reunion was overwhelmed by another celebration: the return to Hespeler of the hundreds of men and women who had served in the Canadian armed forces during the war. The summer of 1946 did see parades and parties in honour of those who had served, but the official reunion was postponed until 1947. Some of the History Group members recalled how the organization of that event began:

K. Buller: Phin couldn't have organized the Old Boys' Reunion in 1947 all by himself.
Archie: No. The group, the BB Boys would have a lot to do with it.
Bill: Yeah, Jack Courtnay would be in on it, and the Kohli's.
Gail: What's 'BB Boys' stand for?
Archie: Well, a 'bunch of bad boys.' No, the 'Bachelor Boys' Club.'
Francis: That Bobby Phin wasn't a bachelor!
Archie: It was a closed club. They gambled every Friday night.

The people referred to no longer bear the names of 'founding fathers' – Forbes, Parmabaker. But they are related in spirit, and sometimes by blood, to those forebears. Bob Phin, for instance, was a pharmacist by profession but is best remembered for his voluntary 'good works.' He organized community clubs and led service organizations in doing much of what the family-run companies had done in the earlier era. The small group of local business owners known as the 'BB Boys' organized complex volunteer support for the Old Boys' Reunions in 1926 and 1947. Phin and these four or five friends also supported and facilitated churches and service clubs in their charitable activities (Harvey 1966, 51).

Thus, despite the gradual erosion of face-to-face influence, the stories that we heard about groups such as the 'BB Boys' showed us that certain small-town traditions persevered in Hespeler well into the postwar period. The leadership cliques defined by informal gatherings such as poker circles operated much as they always had. They made certain strategic decisions on their own, without a lot of wide-ranging consultation, and then set about mobilizing the townspeople to implement them. This process was oligarchic, but the decisions that resulted were not necessarily sinister or oppressive. The elite groups were well in touch with the spirit of the town and bound to its populace in many different ways, both economically and socially.

The 1947 reunion was widely remembered as the best of the five held in Hespeler prior to 1996. The town council stood firmly behind it, as did the mill owners. In the flush of victory, Hespeler savoured the apex of its heyday, thanks to cooperation among the private (corporate) and public (municipal) sectors.

The event was reputed to have attracted over 100,000 people during its run. One of the organizers wrote to a local editor to explain this phenomenon: 'It is the people of Hespeler, Mr. Templin. You know the kind I mean. The friendly people. The kind that have a moment to pass the time of day: who want to help you get along and are prepared to help you by supporting local projects, by planning new schools, new arenas and all the things that go to make up a good town. The people who are glad, and proud, to be on civic bodies, on committees sponsoring such shows as the Old Boys Reunion. More than ten percent of Hespeler's population are working on this big event. And the other ninety percent are doing their bit too' ('Hespeler's 100,000 Friends' 1947).

By 1966, the Old Boys' Reunion had only a shell of the old industrial base to call on for support. Nevertheless, the town council rallied to produce a fourth reunion. It was a game attempt to revitalize the glory of a town whose economic fate was in decline. Percy Harvey took the lead in the struggle to uphold the community's traditions, as owner of a local business, mayor, and county commissioner. The 1966 reunion was a bit smaller than earlier efforts, but Percy was proud of his achievement, as were the local media.

No one could deny, however, that Hespeler had seen better times. Big events such as the reunions were getting harder to do, without the industry that had sustained the town's boom times. The 'BB Boys' were past their prime, without a cohesive group to replace them. Many people were convinced that 1966 was the last reunion. As we see in the next chapter, however, the strongly symbolic memories of past reunions came to be the foundation on which a revived sense of community could be built.

5

The Great Hespeler Reunion

The Roots of the Reunion

The beginning of the year 1995 brought many changes to the Company of Neighbours. Our source of funding shifted from the Donner Canadian Foundation and Ontario's Ministry of Community and Social Services to the Trillium Foundation. Our data gathering and analysis, reported in chapters 3 and 4, had led us to feel that we understood the community's central concerns and traditions. We sensed that we might be on the brink of the 'action phase' of our project. Our 'narrative community' was much stronger than it had been when the project began, and we felt that the reshaping of the community narrative might be at hand.

It was not clear, however, what form that new story might take. The local history–oriented memorabilia centre at the site office, the 'Evenings in the Park,' and the dialogues with students at Hespeler's schools were the most visible outcomes of our work in the community to that point. Our strategic decision to facilitate, rather than direct, the action phase of the project implied some risks. Would the interest and enthusiasm of our small group spread or dissipate? The answer came that spring, as the voice of Hespeler's traditions made itself heard loud and clear.

As part of the process of community feedback, John Jeffery and Ken Banks arranged to be the speakers at a Cambridge Rotary Club meeting in late March 1995. Reflecting on the exploratory phase of the project, they summarized some of the themes that had emerged. They talked about the loss of a sense of community in Hespeler and about how the apparent incapacity to stage another Old Boys' Reunion symbolized that loss to many people. Towards the end of the meeting, a Hespeler-born Rotarian, David Mitten, stood up and said: 'The last Reunion was held in

1966, let's hold one in 1996.' Despite their initial reservations, John and Ken said that they knew many local people who would like to try. John, Ken, and David called everyone whom they could think of who might be interested in reviving the Hespeler Reunion and held a meeting on 1 May 1995, at the Company of Neighbours' site office. Eleven people attended.

As recounted to some extent in chapter 4, The Old Boys' Reunions had been massive events that had taken place, roughly every twenty years, between 1906 and 1966. In 1947, as the soldiers returned from the Second World War, a ten-day reunion drew perhaps over 100,000 people. However, local industries and the town council had provided organizational and financial help for the first four reunions. This time, the organizing phase could not depend on sponsorship by a local municipal council or a single dominant industry. But it did have the Company of Neighbours.

The Company of Neighbours began to act as a form of secretariat for the reunion. Joann Woods became secretary of the reunion committee, with David as chair, and Bill Jarrett, a local accountant, as treasurer. At the first meeting, Ken proposed that the committee not overload itself with unnecessary organization. He suggested that it use parliamentary procedure if needed, and that it could even become incorporated. But, in following our philosophy of informal organization, the reunion should not waste energy on those things until lack of formal organization became a problem. In other words, at the beginning we suggested that the reunion committee be organized along the lines of a 'hardly worth mentioning' group (see chapter 3).

Working within this consensus model, everyone agreed that if David was willing to take the chair, the others would support him. They also agreed that if it became evident that they needed an election, they could hold one at that point. Frankly, many of us expected that the municipality, or at least insurance companies, would force the committee to take on contractual forms of legal responsibility, but those anticipated barriers proved to be purely hypothetical. The individuals involved, their standing in the community, and the fact that they were backed by a popular movement gradually became familiar to those in authority. With little formal power to award, and no profits to be made by individuals, the group earned the trust that was afforded it. It was, after all, doing something that was beneficial to the municipality (and its efforts to promote tourism), at virtually no direct cost to it.

The relationship between the Company of Neighbours and the Great Hespeler Reunion Committee was informal, enmeshed, and cordial. The Company of Neighbours gradually separated itself from the administra-

tive support of Wilfrid Laurier University, so as to become more autonomous and self-sustaining. In September 1995, we had formed a steering
committee for the Company of Neighbours that would make autonomy
possible. By late October, the funds were in a local bank branch, with
project participants as signing authorities. Virtually everyone involved
in the Company of Neighbours' steering committee also had some role in
the Great Hespeler Reunion.

Beginning in the autumn of 1995, the Company of Neighbours' monthly
meetings heard reports on the progress of the reunion. Sadly, in late
September John Jeffery suddenly resigned his responsibilities for cultural programs on the reunion committee. We were all baffled until, in
October, we heard that he was seriously ill. Ken Buller temporarily
assumed the treasurer's role, but on 30 October we were informed that
John only had six weeks to live. On 5 November he died in hospital.

In addition to his work with the 'Evenings in the Park' and school
liaison, John had engineered formation of the Company of Neighbours'
steering committee. He was enthusiastic about establishing local autonomy, but he had been more quiet in the last few months, saying that
he 'felt different.' His illness was a great shock to us, but we were
determined to honour his commitment to spreading knowledge of local
history, so we carried on.

Ken was asked to speak at a moving memorial service at John's school.
Joann placed a poignant reflection in her field notes on 3 January 1996,
reflecting our sense of persevering through our sadness: 'The past couple
of months have been very hard here, with the passing of John Jeffery, my
favourite Aunt, and even Kelsey, Gail's beloved little dog. We also have
been very busy with the reunion and the Santa Claus Parade. The Company of Neighbours had a calendar made of local historic scenes, it sold
very well.' Ken's mother, Charlotte Kinsman Banks, also died at age
ninety later in January. All in all it was a difficult time, but the success of
our projects, the reunion's increasing momentum, and the growing
number of people involved sustained us and forced us on.

As 1995 drew to a close, the Company of Neighbours was becoming a
hub of activity, with the reunion and other community activities acting
like the spokes of a wheel in relation to their common driving energy
source. Russell Bygrave had run the local Santa Claus Parade for sixteen
years prior to December 1995. But Russell had several heart attacks and
was in hospital just weeks before the parade was to take place. A loose-
knit network of Company of Neighbours and Optimist Club members,
led by Russell's wife, Peg, did the preparations for the parade. Russell

(sometimes known informally as 'the mayor of Hespeler') also relied on support from his fellow Optimists. We noticed that anything that they did was done quietly, so as not to take away from Russell's achievement of single-handedly setting up and running a parade with over ninety units every year.

Over the winter, the Company of Neighbours became the official information centre for the reunion. Our phone/fax number and e-mail address went out on all reunion promotional material. We were made directly responsible for the historical displays that were to be at some of the events leading up to the reunion and at the Welcome Centre. Those tasks were compatible with keeping the memorabilia centre staffed by volunteers, and renewing its stock of pictures and artefacts. Soon, many of the reunion's key volunteers were using the site office as an operations centre, which gave Joann a great deal of support. She wrote in her field notes on May 18: 'In the office this morning to wait for an Optimist member to come and get the keys for the cash register (that they borrowed for a reunion fund raiser) so I thought this would be a good time to write down some things that have been going on around the Company of Neighbours: A LOT.' Apparently, she had no time to elaborate.

Developmental Stages

As should be clear by now, there was no grand organizational blueprint that the Company of Neighbours or the reunion committee followed. In some ways, this became our greatest strength. We relied on participants' good will and personal relationships, rather than on elaborate structures of committees and subcommittees, to get things done. In retrospect, we can see that the reunion organized itself into what we characterize as five stages:

1 'Auld Lang Syne'
2 'Bravado'
3 'Cautiously Confident'
4 'Hespeler Sure Knows How to Party'
5 'I Don't Believe We Did It ... Now What?'

1 'Auld Lang Syne'

The first meeting of the reunion committee on 1 May 1995 attracted only the four organizers and some of their friends and relatives. This small group initially decided to spread the idea and see if people responded to the notion of a reunion in 1996. For the time being, David Mitten agreed to chair the group, and those present who belonged to service clubs said that they would talk with other members about potential support. Everyone also agreed to sound out friends and neighbours and bring volunteers to the next meeting.

Service club members soon reported that there was a lot of interest around town and that the Legion and churches should also be contacted. The group decided to distribute a questionnaire asking people to volunteer according to their interests and to list events that they would expect to be held at the reunion. We began to see the Company of Neighbours performing exactly as we had hoped: coordinating existing community structures and acting as a catalyst for mobilization of existing public-minded groups, rather than attempting to create new organizations with their own plans.

Many people came to just one meeting, for what the research team called 'Auld Lang Syne' – a last look at a (probably) futile attempt to regain the local autonomy of old. Some left, their curiosity satisfied, but many more stayed when they saw what was happening. Penny Thompson, a graphic designer recruited by David, started to gather local artists' renditions of Hespeler scenes and symbols for use in promoting the reunion. Plans were set to call all the clubs and institutions of Hespeler together in June, in order to garner commitments from local members and to recruit volunteers to take on essential tasks.

About forty people attended the community meeting held in the Old Scout Hut on the sweltering evening of 19 June 1995. Young and old, men and women, the curious and the committed came out. David Mitten talked to them about the reunion in a low-key manner. He then asked those present for their ideas and, finally, for their commitment. The representatives of the Canadian Legion offered their members to help with the sports and some social events. Some male Optimists suggested that they could help with funds and sponsorship. Even the leaders of the two competing seniors' groups spoke in a civil manner to each other and agreed that they could cooperate to produce some events. Eighteen more people joined the reunion committee that night, and the meeting was considered a success.

The reunion committee grew: by 11 July it consisted of thirty-one people, from old Hespeler families and new, and from a wide variety of occupations and areas of town. Despite the wide representation on this committee, however, it still was not taken seriously by many of the people in authority in Cambridge. Evidence of its coming of age came in September, when Helen Scott-Wallace and Bill Brown joined the committee. Helen was on the cultural affairs staff of the City Parks and Tourism Board, and Bill was the local member of the Cambridge city council. Somewhat to our surprise, these officials did not try to dominate the proceedings, but participated like all the others. They gave added confidence to the group by providing details on city permits and insurance issues as they arose in meetings. Their presence also reassured the group that it was not seen by the authorities as a runaway bunch of renegades.

Privately, however, people who had been involved in earlier reunions were still concerned that we might be fooling ourselves. Funding was a particular worry. At one of our recorded meetings, Bill O'Krafka commented:

Bill: I don't know, Ken. It takes a lot of money, and we always had the town council to pick up any deficit. The last time they had a $6,000 loss, because they printed too many reunion books, and the town council covered it. You don't have that this time, and the big companies are gone that sponsored everything. Where will you come up with the money? I'd love to see this happen, as you know, but I honestly have to tell you that I'm worried.

Other participants showed that they were well aware of the history of community support:

John G.: Back in 1966, when we had corporate sponsorship, there were all the big companies. They were able to support us. And now we're worried about where we're going to get a lot of it.

Lary: In 1966, in the last reunion, and in '47, I think, there were industries that were in Hespeler which had people seconded to the committee [i.e., released from work].

Clearly the reunion would need a solid financial base, and fundraising was the first serious task taken on. It got off to a reasonably good start as we forged alliances with local service clubs. The Hespeler North Optimists (Women's) Club, the Hespeler Optimists (Men's) Club, and the Cambridge North Rotary Club, the group that had launched David Mitten's idea, pledged thousands of dollars. But the effort soon stalled, as there was not much confidence that local business and industry would help in times of fiscal retrenchment. Also worrying was the fact that the city had been hit with a 49 per cent cut to its provincial allotment in November, so a grant from its treasury was not guaranteed. Even so, many felt that this was not a major problem, as we had proudly stated that we would not depend on governments to fund the reunion.

The real hero of the fund-raising phase was Harold Markel, a son of Hespeler who had made good in his own manufacturing and marketing businesses. Assuming a key role in the fund-raising effort, Harold came up with a strategy that was predicated on no possible deficit. We were to raise money to pay all the bills before the reunion took place. Any money made during the reunion itself would be surplus and would be donated to community works after the reunion was over. Harold set up a sponsorship plan that recognized major donors publicly and established an organizational structure for the sale of advertising in the 'Reunion book.' He, Bill Jarrett, and David Mitten then drew on their marketing and business contacts to hold a press conference and kick off the campaign.

To many in February 1996, our goal of raising $60,000 over the next four months made us sound truly out of touch with reality. But the necessary organization was there, and the money started to trickle and then to pour in. In March, Zehr's markets, whose headquarters are in Hespeler, took out a major sponsorship. John Gunther spearheaded the effort to sell ads in the *Reunion Book*, and revenues began to flow. Stan Jones, who had published school yearbooks, set up the layout for the *Reunion Book* in a manner that looked effortless. Penny Clemens, Penny Thomson, and Christine Boyle showed great talent in graphics design and public relations.

Within a couple of months, the committee had raised $19,000 in advertising sales and $30,000 in sponsorships. Sensing that the reunion was for real, the city also chipped in $5,000, insurance coverage, and free permits and services. Harold, the visionary, had been right, though he was loath to take any credit for what he did. The action phase of our project thus began to take shape in ways that we would not have predicted and (happily) could not control.

Not everything was going as we would have liked it, however. There were occasions when we began to notice an uncomfortable gender split among the volunteers. Many who attended early meetings were middle-aged women, but most of them did not return. Whether they felt dominated by their male contemporaries in the group and went home in frustration, or decided that this was just so much bravado on the part of the fading old boys in the group, we do not know, but we were sorry to lose their participation.

In other areas, however, the presence of female volunteers was more visible. There was active recruitment of people with specific skills for the committee, and several of the key players recruited were women. Sometimes, efforts to recruit women ended up netting a man, as the following story relates:

Jim: Last November I was up at John's drinking beer. I know John would never get involved, you could never twist his arm to get involved in anything. I asked his wife to join, Beverly, who said she had enough to do. Then John said, 'Maybe I'll come out.'

Through incidents such as this, we began to realize that the 'hardly worth mentioning' model of organization might be open to male domination. It encourages a great deal of chaos, over-talking, and storytelling as a way of doing the business at hand. A room full of 'old boys' can be daunting to an outsider. We noticed that some insensitive things were said, and rude jokes or allusions were made by men in some of these meetings. One could see how it was difficult for the women to stand up to men who were used to being dominant. When women took men to task on the committee, there was tension and sometimes nervous laughter, but other men and women in the group would usually assert the women's right to speak. In the end, only five women stayed with the reunion committee, but they were central to its success, and we considered this an advance from the strict male dominance of the past.

The 'Old Boys' Reunion' thus became the Great Hespeler Reunion, and not only in name. Its form and function started to shift away from the preferences of older male authorities in the content and conduct of community action. Thus we had started by looking nervously to the past, then realized that there were past practices that we could not or did not want to replicate. In the end, we pushed our way over those hurdles and started to make our own organizational path (see Horton and Freire 1990).

2 'Bravado'

As plans for the reunion progressed, the effort gained momentum and attracted enthusiastic new participants. In some ways, the committee was sustained by little more than its own bravado. But within that brashness was the knowledge that belief in a purpose is the first step towards concrete results.

There was also growing evidence that the leadership style that we were trying to promote through the Company of Neighbours was starting to catch on. In September 1995, in the early stages of the reunion, Penny Thomson had designed four logos which she brought to a meeting for the group's consideration. They were all gorgeous, and professionally executed, but the traditionalists wanted to use the town's old symbol of the beehive. They were not attracted to the modern versions, which looked like cartoon bees buzzing around a kind of inflated hive. The group was almost equally divided, but David did not force a choice, and a compromise was reached. Penny's symbols would be used for posters, T-shirts, and the letterhead. The traditional beehive would appear in the parade and other events where it was deemed more appropriate. The old and new were used interchangeably throughout the development of the event, with no perceptible confusion resulting.

The first draft of the program for the reunion was passed around at the 2 September 1995 meeting. It would eventually develop into that shown in Figure 5.1. Almost thirty events were agreed upon but the expanding scale of the event created a somewhat unreal atmosphere. There were no budgets and what seemed to be an almost endless amount of time before we actually had to do anything about staging the planned events. The dates were set for 5, 6, and 7 July 1996, so we ploughed ahead with plans, regardless of the obstacles.

For the residents of a little town that had almost lost its identity, closing down main street for several days, holding fireworks displays in the park, and conducting a huge street dance were 'empowering' concepts. Together, Hespelerites committed themselves to making these events happen. Such tasks as having a banner made (a donation of the Business Improvement Association) and getting it installed over the main street were small victories. 'This is really going to happen,' we nervously told each other in the bars, and others nodded solemnly and offered to buy us drinks.

Andre Watteel, owner of the Olde Hespeler Bar and Grill, was one of the first business people to step in and actually help us as things got rolling. If the initial organization had highlighted some gender issues in town, hints of class divisions began to appear with Andre's participation. The Olde Hespeler had many patrons who were involved with motorcycling, and Andre had a reputation for being able to handle any unseemly behaviour that might erupt. His support was met with mixed emotions by the committee. David and the middle-class members were slightly shocked and somewhat fearful, for they had never set foot in his place.

FIGURE 5.1
The Great Hespeler Reunion of '96 – Preview of Events

It is in great tradition that we present The Great Hespeler Reunion of 1996. We are looking forward to three exciting, fun filled days. This listing is an overview of what we have planned, please watch for future information detailing these events. Please contact The Company of Neighbours, if you would like further information, 14 Queen Street East, Cambridge Phone/Fax (519) 651-0032.

• • • • • • • • • •

FRIDAY JULY 5

Welcome Centre Opens for Registration – Johnson Centre
Carnival – Forbes Park
Hespeler Fire Station – Open House
Mini-Reunions
Casino – (Hespeler Optimist) Beehive Hall
Reunion '96 Opening Ceremonies – Hespeler Arena
Shamrock 'Oldtimer' Hockey Game

• • • • • • • • • •

SATURDAY JULY 6

Queen Street mall; Adam – Cooper, Tannery – Adam Street.
Welcome Centre Open
Breakfast in the Mall
Arts & Craft Vendors – Queen Street Mall
Carnival – Forbes Park
Live Bands & Entertainment – Queen Street Mall
Family Swim – Johnson Centre
Judging – Beard Growing Contest

Reunion '96 Parade – Queen Street
Fire Station Open House – Tannery Street
Mini-Reunions
Strawberry Social – St. Andrew's Hespeler Presbyterian Church
Antique Car Show – Town Hall
Helicopter Rides – Guelph Ave
Hot Air Balloon Rides – Johnson Centre
3 on 3 Basket Ball – Hespeler Baptist Church Adam Street
Pony Rides – Street
3-6-9 Tournament – Hespeler Playfair Bowl
Pool & Darts Tournament – Old Hespeler Hotel
Food Booths – Queen Street Mall
Barbecue – Ted Wake Lounge
Teen Dance – Jacob Hespeler High School
Street Dance – Queen Street Mall

• • • • • • • • • •

SUNDAY JULY 7

Welcome Center Open
Brunch in the Mall – Queen Street Mall
Carnival – Forbes Park
Mini-Reunions – Check Individual Listing
All Day Sporting Events
Soap Box Derby (Big Brothers) – Rife Ave
California Cuties Baseball – Victoria Park
3 on 3 Basket Ball – Hespeler Baptist Church Adam Street
Skull Races – Speed River above the falls
Canoe Races – Speed River above the falls
Sky Divers – Victoria Park Before Concert
Closing Ceremonies Concert and Fireworks Display

When Andre came to a meeting and offered to run a beer tent during the reunion, there was a mixture of excitement and desperation in the room. In contrast to some committee members, who felt that the family atmosphere of the reunion was at risk, the working-class members felt right at home at the Olde Hespeler and saw Andre as their friend and supporter.

Once again, the offer was not voted on, and another potential crisis passed. By December, darts and pool tournaments were being sponsored by the Olde Hespeler as fund-raisers, but disappointingly few people took part.

Some of the early organizational efforts for the reunion thus exposed tensions along lines of gender and class but also showed that the participants were capable of resolving (or at least ignoring) those tensions. Similar tensions were revealed in the reaction to Russell Bygrave's announcement that he had accepted a parade entry, and a donation, from the Mirage, a local establishment featuring exotic dancers. Images of a float featuring scantily clad dancers immediately filled some people's minds. Many members of the committee felt that they could not countenance such a display against public morality. Others argued that the Mirage employees were as much a part of the community as the other participants. Many sat on their hands when it came to a vote, but again a compromise was achieved: it was agreed that there would be a float in the parade, but that the dancers must be fully clothed.

Russell had only begun, however. His next idea was to include a celebrity from 'The Young and the Restless' TV soap opera, to be paid to ride in the parade. Some middle-class members ridiculed this proposal, but David found that there was a groundswell of solid support for it from the working-class members and their backers. In the end, the committee authorized an expensive contract for the presence of 'Joshua Morrow' in, and for an hour after, the parade. This turned out to be another astute business move, as the involvement of this celebrity would draw thousands of fans to the reunion.

Some members of the reunion committee were definitely 'thinking big,' and their bravado was paying off. But there was also some swift and subtle problem-solving behind the scenes, by some of the key players. For instance, we learned that in January 1996, before the municipal grant was approved, key members of city staff had given David a bad scare by informing him that the reunion would not be covered by city insurance. David kept this information to himself and went through political channels to unblock a possible bottleneck. The relief was audible in his voice the night he called to say, 'You can let people know that the city's public-events blanket insurance policy *will* cover the reunion.' Perhaps that was the day that the reunion volunteers started to change from nearly pure bravado to calm confidence in their abilities and achievements.

Programs began to gain momentum as well. Lary Turner, a veteran postal worker who had volunteered to look after entertainment, and John

Trothen, the mall manager who undertook the broad mantle of 'logistics,' were moving ahead competently to arrange the intricate events. Harold Markel told us to rent a 'parade of armoured trucks' to bring in the cash that he predicted would be raised. During the winter, regular post-meeting gatherings for beer and chicken wings began, at which the details for implementation of decisions made at the meeting were worked out in a more informal atmosphere. Several spouses of committee members joined in these gatherings, and some of them ended up working during the reunion itself.

3 'Cautiously Confident'

By April 1996 money from sponsorships and advertising in the reunion book was pouring in. Members of the Company of Neighbours, and of the various reunion committees, began to feel more sure of themselves and of their plans. The city's grant of $5,000 (more than we had asked for) arrived, and Bill Jarrett was walking around town with a smile. Negotiations for permits for the parade and the street vendors were under way. Planning for the carnival, the helicopter rides, and the fireworks display was ongoing. Parking and security were being worked out by the half-dozen or so volunteers who had taken on that responsibility. In cases where key tasks were not being worked on, people who had been recruited to assist on other areas took over, without much fanfare. Lines of demarcation for organization between tasks became blurred as certain people became aware that they worked well together and that some of their responsibilities overlapped.

For a few weeks David was not certain who was working on what, but by the spring the picture was clearer. In some cases it was small clusters of committee members without a designated leader who took responsibility as necessary. At the bi-weekly committee meetings Lary Turner and John Trothen reported jointly on logistics. Jim Wilson and Stan Jones reported on the reunion book; Jim dealt with its photography, Stan with its copy. Penny Clemens spent long hours on its lay-out but never attended a reunion meeting. Eventually, their small group produced a book that sold almost 3,000 copies. Russell Bygrave ran the parade, with minimal involvement from David, which arrangement worked well. Though they are very different, both realized that the other was making an essential contribution.

The blending of popular culture with more respectable bourgeois culture was absolutely necessary for the success of the reunion. It seemed that art shows, craft fairs, and historical displays were fine with everyone. But the working-class people had to fight some resistance for the street dance and for the presence of 'their' celebrities in the parade. Experience showed that they were right, in terms of popularity and participation. Band concerts and fireworks were also sure-fire hits to which everyone agreed. But some events (like the 'California Cuties' – a softball team in drag) were initially considered to be beyond the pale but then proved to be very popular. In the end, the reunion largely transcended class tastes, with most people thoroughly enjoying all the events.

There was still a sense that 'it's only us, can we really do this?' Some participants were waiting for a devastating, insurmountable problem to surface, but none did. The fireworks company went bankrupt the week before we were to pay our deposit, so David contracted with the largest company in Canada. Next, we could not identify the legal owners of the field behind the arena where the fireworks were to be ignited. We spoke to a city official, who asked, 'Just who, then, is going to protest this use of the land? By the time they figure out who has the right to protest, the fireworks will be over, and you'll be long out of there.'

The reunion was by this time a quasi-public event. The reunion committee had no official authority to do anything, so other authority was either suspended temporarily or appropriated on its behalf as needed. We began to recognize that our cohesiveness, and our of purpose, created their own kind of authority. Two weeks before the reunion we gave ourselves a party at the Olde Hespeler Bar and Grill to celebrate publication of the reunion book. It was a huge success, with everyone, regardless of background, celebrating for hours. Gender and class differences were not forgotten, but a mutually acceptable way to surmount them was in evidence that evening.

The week before the reunion was terrifying. 'What if it rains?' we thought. 'What if we're fooling ourselves and nobody shows up?' 'What if gangs of kids disrupts the street dance like they did the week before in Quebec City?' We did not ask each other just exactly what the insurance policy covered, because there was nothing we could do about it now, but suddenly we felt responsible for what was about to happen. We *were* responsible – there were no two ways about it. We had taken on the responsibility along with the authority.

But this was the Great Hespeler Reunion. Just as it did not belong to the city or to business it did not belong to the committee or to the Company of Neighbours. It now belonged to the community.

4 *'Hespeler Sure Knows How to Party!'*

The research team members had not experienced a community reunion before, and we were caught somewhat by surprise by the phenomenon as it unfolded. We expected something like a Canada Day celebration or a county fair, but it was far, far more. The History Group worked for days to assemble displays of photographs and artefacts representing different periods of Hespeler's past. These formed the backdrop of the Welcome Centre. For three days, people at the centre would eye each other, circle around, and then say, 'Is it you, is it really you?' – followed by hugs and shrieks of pleasure. People came from all over the world to see the town and friends from an earlier time in their lives. People from Scotland and Australia came back to reflect on their life with old acquaintances. Others, who arrived just for the parade or the canoe races, watched the joyous mini-reunions on the streets of Hespeler with amazement and pleasure. Carnival tents and rides began to sprout in Forbes Park, where our 'Evenings in the Park' had been held in summers past.

Friday night featured an old-timer's hockey game, with members of the 'Shamrocks' teams from several past decades. At half-time, the reunion committee received its only moment of public recognition. The mayor of Cambridge and other local politicians appeared on the dais, now happy to share in the glory, but David did a wonderful job of keeping the speeches and presentations short and sweet. The arena was packed, standing room only, and the feeling began to grow that the reunion was going to be a great success.

Saturday, 6 July, the second day of the reunion, dawned sunny and warm. Queen Street was closed to accommodate two blocks of arts and crafts stalls, with wandering clowns and performers. A bandstand in front of city hall showcased local talent of every description. The carnival midway filled Forbes Park, connecting the Welcome Centre with the downtown core. That afternoon, a parade of ninety-odd floats and displays wound through the packed streets of Hespeler under sunny skies. Russell confided later, 'You know, when we left the Zehr's parking lot I was kinda scared. I did not see any people. But when we made that turn onto Queen Street and I seen the thousands of 'em there, well, y'know, I got a little bit of a tear in my eye.' As the last of the floats passed, spectators spontaneously joined in behind, filling the streets from curb to curb.

That night, another in an amazing series of events occurred: the street dance, featuring the Silver Saddle Band. Lary remembered this group as one of Hespeler's star products, a country-rock band of the mid-1970s that had achieved considerable regional success. It had split up years earlier, with members starting families and following other careers. Lary hunted them down, however, one by one and cajoled them into getting together again. Once they strapped on their guitars, a momentum began that could not be stopped. What better symbol of the Great Hespeler Reunion than a reunited Hespeler band? Nervous and trembling as they took the stage for their first concert in some twenty years, they were greeted with tumultuous applause and enthusiastic support. For the next three hours, their new and old music provided the soundtrack for an outdoor party that featured people of all ages and backgrounds. For us, there was not much to do during this time, but to watch in awe and respect what the folks of Hespeler had accomplished.

On Sunday, an ecumenical service jammed the largest church in town. A men's quartet that had been together for over fifty years sang to great effect, and the faith communities merged for several hours in harmony. In the evening 'The California Cuties,' a men's travelling softball team in drag, played a team of local fire-fighters. It was sexist, mildly offensive to some, slapstick, and hilarious. Several thousand spectators sat stubbornly through spitting rain and threatening thunderheads to watch this fun from an earlier era. Then more bands and soloists started to perform in the city's portable band shell by the arena. A team of reunion-committee members sold hundreds of sausages donated by Schneider's, a local company.

The Great Hespeler Reunion finale featured an expertly edited video of reunion scenes, played on a giant screen for the crowd of 8,000. Mark Girer and his staff had worked through the day to produce the tape. They had to hold the screen in place manually during the presentation because of technical difficulties. The final version, featuring interviews with participants as well as scenes of the reunion, joined an earlier production on 'Hespeler and Its Reunions' as a fund-raising item for sale through the Company of Neighbours.

There was one more thing that was very important about Sunday night. The arena, site for these closing ceremonies, is on the edge of one of the new housing projects in Hespeler. These are home to the 'Mississauga West' commuters, who know and usually care little about the place where they live. Thousands of them, however, walked over to the park, curious after the traffic jams and parades of the previous day. They brought their children and their coolers and roared their approval of the night's events. The fireworks display lasted until almost eleven p.m., and they applauded and stomped their feet for fifteen minutes after it was all over. Most of them seemed to know that this event was not put on by civic authorities, but was facilitated and organized by their neighbours, some of whom lived in their developments. They bought reunion books and T-shirts by the hundreds that night and went home with a renewed sense of what makes Hespeler such a special place to live.

The reunion and its governance stand as a remarkable tribute to people's ability to organize and even to regulate themselves as appropriate. Andre Watteel had come to a committee meeting in April and offered the services of some 'barmen' or bouncers for security during the reunion, particularly at the street dance. The Reunion Committee declined this offer. It recognized that the street-dance celebrants, far from being inter- lopers, were also part of the community. Any disruption of the event would upset their spouses, parents, children, and possibly friends. Andre, and Ernie of Ernie's Roadhouse down the street, also had their reputa- tions as responsible bar owners to worry about; they needed to keep peace in the community, to *not* be the source of any disruption. A form of informal social contract had to be achieved, without direct negotiations among the parties to the agreement. Word went out that the committee was contracting only a few off-duty regional police officers for security. Everyone who attended had a responsibility to keep the peace.

At the event, we had a small group of voluntary security people and St John's Ambulance volunteers. Between them they diffused a few poten- tially explosive situations with the help of police and dealt effectively with several people who fell ill during the parade. Overall, we estimate that well over fifty thousand people attended over the weekend, with about thirty thousand at the parade and some nine thousand at the street dance, with reasonable order maintained throughout. All day Saturday, organizers greeted one another with grins and the frequent observation that 'Hespeler sure knows how to party!' This was confirmed by the rather copious amounts of alcohol being consumed. The proprietors of the licensed premises, Andre, Ernie, and the Canadian Legion, deserve a great deal of credit for their management, but members of the public generally obeyed the law without being forced to. For the most part, they drank in the licensed spots, as evidenced by the fact that all of those spots, including the bowling alley, ran out of beer, wine, and liquor on Saturday night. Some of the younger people were a bit disruptive at several points, but Ken Buller told a story that showed the commitment of local people to make this event work:

K. Buller: After the dance was over I was standing with a friend of mine, watching people milling around. It was kind of nice, and out of the corner of my eye I saw a flurry of activity up by the library. My friend and I ran up to see what was happening. It was a pigpile of teenagers, some piled on one kid, and others trying to pull fighters apart. My friend, who is very big and knows how to handle himself, waded in, picked up one fighter at a time, set them down again, looked them in the eye and said 'Stay there or I'll hurt you.' By the time the cops arrived, my friend and I, and the security volunteers, had things under control.

To some extent, the reunion committee laid out the parameters of the activity that constituted the reunion, and virtually all of the 50,000-plus people who attended knew how to conduct themselves within those parameters, and did so. The committee happily 'lost control' of the reunion sometime on Friday night and concentrated on keeping the infrastructure together to serve the public. On Sunday morning, for instance, until about five o'clock, reunion and Company of Neighbours volunteers, aided by city staff and machines, finished cleaning up the street.

5 *'I Don't Believe We Did It ... Now What?'*

Important as it was, facilitating a community celebration was not the original intention of the Company of Neighbours. After the reunion, we faced the dilemma of how to convert the renewed awareness of commonality into a more permanent predilection towards community. We also wanted to see if these cultural motivators would 'bleed over' into social supports that would address the needs that we had identified in the exploratory phase. Once the reunion was over, the need for the committee was obviated, but members wanted to carry on. On 23 July 1996, we held a 'debriefing' for many of the organizers, at which we discussed our concerns.

Marshall: What I'd like to know is – some of you may like to speculate a bit – what do you think is going to happen in the future, as a result of the Great Hespeler Reunion?
John T.: I think that it's already started. Because there's people already now, in this room, there's a task force to start an open air-market, within the Hespeler

core area. We're working along with the 'Common Futures' people out of Cambridge, and we've had a couple of meetings already. We've already created a spin-off as a result that we've had from the reunion. I'm sure that there are people in this room who would like to stay on the bandwagon, with its chicken wings and beer, and have an open-air market. Stay on and meet weekly for chicken wings and beer. So I think from that aspect, if the reunion did not exist ... we would not have the market. If Ken hadn't gotten involved, or I hadn't gotten involved, I'd have still been an outsider. We need to keep the momentum going ... I know I'm going to keep involved, volunteering. You guys have changed my thinking about volunteering. This has been a great experience.

People who had not even considered volunteering before they encountered the Company of Neighbours were not ready to give up the solidarity, the spiritual experience of pulling together for a common goal and doing it well.

Stan: I think that we've shown the whole of Hespeler ...
John G: The rest of Cambridge!
Stan: Well, the rest of Cambridge, and I think a good portion of the rest of Ontario, too, that there's enough talent here, and we've individually shown that, there's a talent for doing various things, and that it's a thing that we've done very well. We let people do their own thing, and we've been able to pull this off as a community. And I think that it has the possibility of a number of spinoffs. For twenty-three years I've sort of sat back, and somebody else has done things in the community, and now I realize that things can be done here in the community and I can do something about it.
Christine: Do you think that we can rename Cambridge 'Hespeler?' [laughter].

Clearly, there was a great sense of accomplishment, but how could we keep it together? In the wake of the reunion, ideas for further community projects proliferated. Three main concepts quickly gained notice: a downtown farmer's market, an annual festival, and restoration of the town's railway station.

The following exchange expresses the fear that nothing can be sustained without an ongoing formal organization. In some ways, this attitude runs counter to our beliefs and our goals for the Company of Neighbours. But it seems to be an ingrained part of Anglo-American civic culture, a facet of our democratic process, that we require committees and plans to get things done. Most important, however, the transcript reveals members' collective determination not to lose the excitement and the momentum of the Great Hespeler Reunion:

Lary: Do you know what I said to my wife when I went home at 11:30 on the Sunday night after the reunion? I said, 'What are we going to do next week?' [Laughter] I'm serious, because that was the feeling I had. I said it at the last meeting: 'I been there, we done it, it's over.' What are we going to do next, right?
Michelle: Now what?
Lary: I get the feeling that there's enough enthusiasm around this table that I don't want to see this end with this meeting, or the last meeting. There's been discussions, I've had discussions with David when he was over and we were having a beer, about maybe scaling it down. Putting on an arts-and-crafts, and entertainment, on the same weekend in Forbes Park, as a Hespeler community thing.
Art: We should have the carnival back.
Lary: We can sit here and reminisce, but unless we decide to do something, and do it in a formal way, so that we make a decision as a committee to say, 'Our next project is going to be this ...' We can talk about Russell's railway station, we can talk about different things, we can spin off into different groups and things, and that's where we will lose it. What we should be doing is keep with this group, that has worked well together as a committee, and say 'OK, this, as a committee, is our next project' – and run it.
K. Banks: We could mould it in with the Company of Neighbours. We're all here.

In many ways, the project ideas and the organizational form of the Company of Neighbours are interlinked. We have discussed a possible 'hub-and-spokes' approach. A large committee, based on the Company of Neighbours, would form the hub, and interest groups the spokes, pitching in on tasks as they need to be done. Clusters of people with the necessary mix of talents and skills would focus on each task, perhaps with some of the more enthusiastic choosing to work on parts of several tasks.

Towards a Better Model

In many ways, the Great Hespeler Reunion was a fulfilment of our hopes for the community. It galvanized a wide-ranging cross-section of the community into positive, collaborative action. People spoke repeatedly of how the informal and friendly organization advocated by the Company of Neighbours had produced committees that worked together in harmony. The enthusiasm generated by the reunion for pursuing other community-oriented projects was palpable among those who had participated.

For all the excitement and hope after the reunion, however, not everything went without a hitch. Class-related differences were partially reconciled, but largely papered over, during the event. Five young women stayed with the project and want to carry on, but gender relations still need great improvement, and racial considerations were not even addressed. Christine rightly took some of the air out of the 'old boys' balloon when she pointed out some difficulties of being a woman in this group.

Christine: I suppose this is going to anger some people, but its true: being a young woman in the community, and sitting around a room full of men ... meant that we were actually staring in the face of old-time Hespeler. And how accepting was old-time Hespeler going to be to young families? Definitely, I feel personally, it was a rough road, but one worth travelling. It definitely improved my personal thick-skinned-ness, that I'm slowly developing, and it was worth the challenge. So, what did I bring to the reunion? A lot of sweat, a lot of heartache, a lot of tears, and a lot of joy. It was worth a year out of my life, and that of my family along with me. Personally, I grew, but in addition to that, I think that, when we first moved here in 1990, Hespeler became our home because it had – because it wasn't Galt, and it wasn't Kitchener. It had, you know, this rough and tough ambience to it, and that's what appealed to us. And becoming involved in the reunion sort of gave us some blood, that we shed into the community, into the growth of our town. I'd never written a poem before in my life, not even to my husband, and I wrote a poem for 'The Book.'
Others: A good one, too!
An excellent poem.
Yes, excellent!
Christine: So when we chose our first home, and our first community to live in, it was a commitment that we made for a long time. And being part of this reunion has made it more of a home than just a place to live.
Others: Well, we love to have you here.
Christine: Well, thank you ...
Others: You belong here, Chris!

This exchange reflects both frustration and success, resistance and acceptance, within the group. Christine confronts the old sexism with the assertiveness of the new generation. The older women with roots in Hespeler stayed away from the reunion-organization process. They probably knew that it would be difficult. But 1996 was different enough that, while it at times was difficult for the young women who came out and confronted the male bastion, they eventually knocked some permanent holes in it, as they took a hand in rebuilding the community their way.

Being from out of town may have been an advantage for Christine and Penny Thompson. They did not have the experience of being silenced by local male friends. This was a phenomenon that we had observed when the older women had joined the older men in the History Group story-telling sessions. The women would struggle to be heard, and when they were ignored, would finally no longer come out to the meetings. Even with the research team trying to hear them out, they would effectively be silenced. We found that we could not restructure something so complex as traditional gender relations in a few meetings. But we also noticed that younger women, raised in a different milieu, were ready and willing to confront the remnants of sexism, and we attempted to assist them whenever we could. In 1997, Christine became the new chair of the Company of Neighbours.

Reflections on the Reunion Process

The Great Hespeler Reunion was, for the most part, a vindication of our belief in a non-directive, facilitative approach. The success of the reunion illustrated the ability of disparate people to work together and to compromise their differences when the project is made more important than the procedures. It showed how class and gender barriers can be reduced (perhaps temporarily) as friendships are made. The challenge for community development is always to sustain the energy for continued change. The best path, the most direct path, is made by many people taking it over and over.

Community development, as we conceive it, is a process that identifies felt needs and facilitates the building of capacities to make local solutions to local problems work. Our model uses ethnography to identify the issues, followed by action-research methods to build organizational capacities that can be used to implement local ideas for a better life. The individual interviews reported in chapter 3, and the historical narrative in chapter 4, provided us with the identification of Hespeler's central traditions, its problems, and some suggested solutions. The research team had a basic picture of community life in Hespeler by the time we finished the first exploratory ethnographic portion of the project. It was this knowledge base that provided the grounds for encouraging the existing community organizations to take new and different initiatives.

The History Group, its efforts to promote interest in local history in the schools, and the Great Hespeler Reunion were what the people who linked themselves with the project wanted to do. The memorabilia centre, the story-telling, and the organizational secretariat were the capacity-building responses that the Company of Neighbours' research team provided for community development. To some extent, these responses were not exactly what we expected, and perhaps not what we would have chosen. But the choice was not ours. A commitment to the action-research paradigm implies, in our view, a commitment to lead only in the information-gathering and reflective stages. The actions must be those chosen by residents, after they have participated in the earlier stages.

The challenge for Hespeler now will be to find the ways and means to continue what the Company of Neighbours has begun. Our funding plan reflects our intention gradually to withdraw and turn over responsibility for maintenance and continuation of the project to local volunteers. The groundwork laid by the Company of Neighbours is very solid, but whether it will be built on, or eroded, remains to be seen.

Conclusion: Implications for Community Development and Action-Research

The process of constructing the story of the Company of Neighbours, and the community of Hespeler, continues today. It is richer and more diverse in its implications for action-research and community development than the outline that we have been able to present here. Drawing out the implications of our qualitative data, and of our experience as participants in this process, is a complex and multifaceted process. The interviews, stories, debates, and field notes that we have organized around a small number of themes have been mediated at every step by us as authors. The full import of the lessons to be learned from these pages must be constructed by our readers and by the people with whom they engage in community action.

It remains only for us to report some of the later activities of the Company of Neighbours as this book went to press, speculate on its future, and make a few closing observations about some of the lessons that we feel we have learned. To the extent that we have been able to organize our discoveries into what might be called a 'theory for experiential learning in the community,' it could be summed up thus: outside-generated, externally imposed structure often *impedes* local autonomy and responsibility for a sustained community effort. By the same token, however, socially engaged action-research, which aims to facilitate rather than to direct such effort, can yield concrete results.

Later Developments

Two weeks after the Great Hespeler Reunion of 1996 ended, the Company of Neighbours hosted a meeting of any and all of the reunion committee members who wanted to carry on with community activities.

This was a follow-up to a gathering that we had held prior to the reunion, on 7 June, at which we partook of the ritual chicken wings and beer. We invited those who attended to consider carrying on with the work of the Company of Neighbours. This courting behaviour was introduced as a way to bridge the loss of momentum that too often happens when a major project ends, even as a huge success. It initiated a series of meetings with members of the reunion committee, to experiment with how we might weave our organizations together.

In chapter 5 we quoted some of the dialogue from the follow-up meeting, including Lary Turner's plea that the group stick together and carry on. We felt that building this bridge would strengthen the Company of Neighbours and make it sustainable, by offering reunion members a way to keep in touch with their new and renewed friends. At that meeting we introduced more openly a version of Murray Ross's (1963) 'wagon-wheel' model of community organization.

With the wagon-wheel, a core organization acts as a catalyst for many potential activities in the community. The 'hub' is the incubator, the enriched environment, for new ideas and strategies. The spokes are the individual initiatives that spring out of the core organization yet continue to contribute to and draw support from the hub. It seemed an appropriate model, as other activities were beginning to flow from the influence of the successful reunion, and community members were being drawn to them. We briefly describe some of those activities and initiatives.

The Hespeler Train Station, an abandoned Canadian National Railways freight depot, had been depicted in a line drawing by local artist Donna O'Krafka for the Company of Neighbours' 1996 calendar. This drawing was adapted to a T-shirt designed for the reunion and generated tremendous sales. Train enthusiast Robert Langdon, now living in Hespeler, was caught up in the wave of nostalgia for this symbol of the old town and called a series of meetings to discuss its presentation.

CN offered to cooperate by selling the building for $500 and renting the land for another $500 per year. Several Company of Neighbours stalwarts joined in and agreed to act as a liaison for the effort. Russell Bygrave began the task of organizing crews of volunteer carpenters, roofers, plumbers, and so on to hold a 'barn raising' to rehabilitate the tumbledown structure. As with so many of the activities begun since the Company of Neighbours arrived in Hespeler, we have not attempted to lead this project, but Robert has invited us to support his organization and take part in the endeavour. The Company of Neighbours now provides office display space for the train-station project.

Russell also recovered sufficiently from his illnesses to organize the 1996 and 1997 Santa Claus Parades, with the help of the Company of Neighbours and various Optimists. The Company of Neighbours contributed a trophy to be awarded to the 'best community float' in 1996 and all future parades.

The Farmers' Market started as an idea shared by John Trothen and an official of the city's 'Our Common Future' project, devised to pull the diverse interests of Hespeler, Preston, and Galt into a common culture of Cambridge. City social workers involved with this initiative expressed concern that Hespelerites seldom had enthusiasm for common efforts with the other components of the city. When the market project was suggested, a community-development worker from the University of Waterloo was suddenly hired by the city to help set it up. John, who has experience as a shopping-mall manager, became chair of the Farmers' Market Committee in August. He then approached the Company of Neighbours with the proposal that we let it share our offices and equipment, in exchange for a contribution to the rent. This project has since found a niche as an organic Farmers' Market.

The Grand River Adventure is a project started by a local rowing club to draw people to the Speed River and to Hespeler. The idea is to purchase rafts and row groups of customers several miles upstream from a point just above the scenic dam beside the American Standard plant. This rowing club ran canoe races on the Speed during the reunion. Public response has been strong. Ken Boyle heads the Speed River Conservation Group, which advocates development of both the Farmers' Market and the rowing project, while continuing to develop scenic walking and biking trails along the Speed.

The Company of Neighbours' History Group carries on, as does its work on book reproductions, print duplications, calendar production, and T-shirt sales. So far it has raised over six thousand dollars per year for the Company of Neighbours. When people come in to the office and see photos of relatives or copies of books and newsletters, they often want copies to take home. The History Group helps get photocopies made, at a cost that provides a small return to the Company of Neighbours. It also sells reunion videos and souvenirs year-round. The photo and book collection was set up and is maintained by Bill O'Krafka and other members of the Group.

Archie Scott has worked with teacher Kelly Main to rejuvenate the history exchange project with Jacob Hespeler Secondary School, and this has found a new energy in connection with a high-tech heritage project known as 'The Watershed Information Systems Environment' (see Mangan 1998). This web-enabled database may provide the starting point for a series of integrated learning experiences, and Marshall is applying for research funding to explore its possibilities further. Local high-school students are also active in other ways: one art student is designing new T-shirts with Jacob Hespeler's image on them; other students spent the summer of 1997 cataloguing the Company of Neighbours' collection of memorabilia.

Recently there has been some talk of establishing a 'proper' museum in Hespeler, but Bill and others close to the History Group suspect that curators and museum professionals would probably not allow residents to lend it books or pictures and take them back at will. They also feel that professional curators would be unlikely to allow visitors to thumb through displays or that they might disapprove of copying valued documents and displaying them on poster board in storefront windows. The people who have created the collection are pretty sure that they would not be welcome, with their limited formal education, as resource people in a 'proper' museum. They say that they and the others will perhaps set up a different kind of museum and find a way for the Company of Neighbours to stay open after the seed funding runs out.

In a move that is perhaps more outside the norm than some of these projects, the Company of Neighbours is also attempting to be a kind of community secretariat. As we envision it, groups with good ideas, but lacking staff and equipment, could use our facilities to promote those ideas. Pooling resources in one office with one part-time staff person and many volunteers makes a lot of sense to us, but we sense some resistance to this idea from the city's power brokers.

Will Success Spoil the Company of Neighbours?

Partly as a result of the success of the reunion and our other activities, we decided in August 1996 to move our office next door, into the larger and brighter premises of the former Mum's Place Restaurant. We formed a task group to meet in September 1996 to discuss our focus and to articulate more clearly the future mission of the Company of Neighbours. Shortly afterward, we heard surprising reports from the committee that was created to dispense reunion profits. Apparently, some members felt that the Company of Neighbours probably had no long-term role in the future of Hespeler. We heard that the Business Improvement Association (BIA), a city-sponsored group that operates as a kind of Chamber of

Commerce and downtown development organization for local merchants, had taken the position that the Company of Neighbours was not likely to survive beyond its start-up funding, despite our many successful fund-raising projects.

When we convened the mission task force on 17 September 1996, David Mitten floated a proposal that essentially would have put the Company of Neighbours under the supervision of the city's Recreation Department, in return for a grant of up to $5,000 per year. Though this might seem like a logical step for a growing community organization, we greeted the idea with skepticism, even dismay. The idea of a mission statement, with written goals and objectives, has been part of textbook-style community organization for over thirty years. But beneath the surface appeal of such structures, the damage that they can do to fluid, autonomous community groups forms the core reason for the innovative nature of our action-research projects.

Though we recognized the need for the Company of Neighbours to take on some form of organization that would allow it to exist after the researchers' participation ended, we also felt that falling into prescribed, conventional organizational structures would begin to crush our efforts to form a narrative community. To fit the Company of Neighbours into the Recreation Commission as an incorporated community association would eliminate local prioritizing of action and make us vulnerable to the uncertainty of annual renewals of city funding. We were discouraged because, after a year of working with the reunion committee as a quasi-autonomous entity, not everyone involved could see this point. We began to feel that though some of our mobilization efforts had succeeded, our community-education goals had not been achieved.

David's view was that, in modern times, an organization needs to have a clear mission statement, and a list of responsible members, in order to get funding. Ken Banks argued that the great success of the Company of Neighbours and the Great Hespeler Reunion lay in the fact that they were not overloaded with unnecessary organizational structure. They had shown a capacity to negotiate the necessary authority when the time came to act responsibly as an organization or to assume community responsibility as situations demanded. In the end, a brief mission state-ment was agreed to, subject to approval of the Company of Neighbours' steering committee. It reads: 'The Company of Neighbours is a catalyst for the promotion of community spirit, through the preservation of Hespeler's culture, tradition, and heritage.' Those in attendance felt that this statement honours the centrality of Hespeler's history, and the work of the History Group, without being overly backward-looking. It also emphasizes the role of the Company of Neighbours as enabling, but not directing, community action.

The move to our new quarters started the day after the task group meeting. Joann, John Trothen, and Bill O'Krafka helped in moving the collection and the stock next door. Art Clarke, a sign-maker by trade, came over with a gorgeous sign, emblazoned with a slogan related to the new mission statement. Ken Boyle donated two gallons of paint, and a painting party was organized for the new premises. People asked Joann every day how they could help, and many pitched in. A modest opening of the new office took place shortly after moving day, in October 1996.

In February 1997, the Company of Neighbours held its first annual general meeting. Most of the people who had been involved in the earlier versions of the steering committee agreed to carry on on the new board. Ken Banks vacated his position as chair, and Christine Boyle was elected to replace him. Marshall Mangan also stepped down as vice-chair, but both he and Ken agreed to stay on as ordinary members of the board. This was a crucial moment in the Company of Neighbours' history, when the organization became completely independent of both outsiders' direction and research-related funding. Equally important was the first regular meeting the following month, which was attended by twenty-one people (a record, not achieved during the researchers' tenure in leadership positions). In one of his favourite phrases, Ken smiled approvingly at the packed house and said, 'Well, looks like we've finally lost control!'

Implications of the Project

The story of the Company of Neighbours has been, for us, an experience by turns exhilarating, exhausting, frustrating, and gratifying. We have learned a great deal, but in general we want to allow the story to speak for itself and to refrain from indulging in too much generalizing. Our project, and our pedagogy, are intentionally descriptive rather than prescriptive. They seek to make available a narrative in which others may find themselves, rather than a dubious formula for success. However, we cannot deny that we have analysed our experiences and attempted to draw some lessons from them. Those lessons include the following.

On the whole, we feel that the Company of Neighbours, as a form of community-development action-research, has been an enormous success. During its existence it has done a great deal, and it is continuing to struggle for local autonomy and self-determination, develop local 'own-ership' through community participation, and explore fluid forms of organization, working towards maximum participation in its democratic processes.

The project achieved the outcomes that it did, in terms of events stimulated and processes initiated, because we began with a fairly well-defined set of value commitments. From these, we developed a research design that was carefully thought out in its principles, but loosely organized in its procedures. We moved from an information-gathering stage based on well-established ethnographic techniques and a problem-oriented concentration, into an action phase, which took us into realms of oral history, community celebration, and consensual democracy that we could never have anticipated. Paradoxically, however, participatory action-research as we conceive it anticipates, and welcomes, unplanned outcomes.

The essence of the Company of Neighbours is what Kimberley Garrett, our program manager from the Trillium Foundation, once called 'the incubator effect' (see Trillium Foundation, 1995). We identify and record the issues that local people are concerned about – the ones that they are talking about over coffee but are not acting on. We provide a supportive atmosphere in which local people can develop a collective response to the issue using local resources. We draw on and focus the strengths of informal groupings. We build on their dialogical interactions to solidify the community narrative and to empower the narrative community. When the indigenous structures have been strengthened and revivified through this process, the professional staff can start to withdraw. Outside funding can be reduced, as a capacity develops for local people to move beyond talk and into action on their own terms.

As we have pursued this path, we have been reminded forcefully of the challenges that such unconventional endeavours face. Efforts to combat the insidious effects of bureaucratic organization are constantly open to criticism as being poorly organized and articulated. Our research paradigm was openly derided by some academic colleagues, and our original funders evidently lost faith. Our own staff and volunteers were frequently baffled by what they saw as a lack of clarity in our stated goals and purposes, despite our repeated attempts to explain our model to them.

Not everyone associated with the project has viewed it as an unalloyed asset to their own plans and ambitions. As the project succeeded at its endeavours and grew in size and influence, it began to attract more attention. Some of that attention was not entirely positive but seemed to be based on a perception that the project had become a competitor with existing service clubs and other community organizations, even though this was never our intention. We eventually crafted positive and constructive relationships with all the existing service organizations and other volunteer groups, but those relationships had to be nurtured cautiously and skilfully.

We discovered through bitter experience that a small project, in a small town, that relies so heavily on a few committed people can be seriously damaged by the loss of one of those people. John Jeffery's sudden death in the autumn of 1995 was not only a terrible loss to his family, his students, and his friends but a near-fatal blow to the educational and youth-oriented programs of the Company of Neighbours.

Formal versus Participatory Democracy

Events of the recent past have shown us that the predilection for bureaucracy is as deeply embedded in Canada's civic culture as is the tendency towards community. The British parliamentary system, which is so ingrained in Canada's concept of democracy, is built on an adversarial system of due process and formal debate (see Macpherson 1977). Its institutions are regarded by many as the only conceivable bastion of democracy, and yet highly organized structures often have the effect of depressing participation, whether in government or in voluntary organizations. In the Company of Neighbours, we sought to develop structures that would permit and encourage widespread direct participation. As Macpherson points out, 'Low participation and social inequality are so bound up with each other that a more equitable and more humane society requires a more participatory political system' (94). The common fixation on parliamentary style ignores the less structured forms of consensus-building that have prevailed for centuries in many Aboriginal societies and in less formal assemblages of people.

It may be that at national and provincial levels of governance, a rule-governed, representative system of elected officials is necessary to protect the diverse interests at stake and to prevent the corruption and undermining of the system. But as one moves towards the local sphere, more direct and informal styles of democracy are feasible. At meetings of the Company of Neighbours, and of the reunion committee, votes rarely took place, and if they did, the results were frequently unanimous. The level of consensus generated from our frequent dialogues and the sense of common purpose that arose were gratifying results of our approach to community-building. Yet we were never able to generate a complete sense of ease with these processes among everyone in attendance or a conviction that they would serve for the long term.

We have learned that, for many Canadians, lack of structure implies impermanence, and they can tolerate looser forms of organization only for so long. When we first encountered this perception, we saw it as a failure in our roles as convenors of an experiential learning experiment. More recently, however, as we have withdrawn from leadership roles, the model has acquired greater legitimacy within the community and among civic authorities. Perhaps we should have expected and anticipated this reaction.

Despite the setbacks, we have carried on, constantly inspired by the responsiveness and dedication of the people who did understand our commitment to a vision of rejuvenated community networks and a genuinely open and participatory process. The strength that we drew from becoming part of their narrative community, and of their community narrative, sustained us through many difficult times. We discovered that narrative approaches to community organization can work to bond people in a secure set of relationships. As they experience each other, they can appreciate what each can contribute to tasks that they may take on. Trust is earned in this process, as is intimacy, and reinforcement of these bonds dispels alienation.

Through dialogue among ourselves, and with our reflexive groups, we began to articulate our analytic themes as well as ways ahead for the project. As the Company of Neighbours' activities moved from small groups, to school-liaison activities, to 'Evenings in the Park,' and on to the Great Hespeler Reunion, we saw a steadily growing sense of self-esteem and autonomous authority emerge within the community, to which we could always return to renew our own.

In a society that shackles local responsibility to a requirement of ownership or membership in formal organizations, open membership is difficult to maintain. We saw the members of the Hespeler Reunion Committee take responsibility for things that needed to be done, without being officially designated as the chairs or owners of the efforts. The whole committee sensed its responsibility for the reunion – for public safety, comfort, and enjoyment. As a result, the community contributed to its own safety (by not being bawdy in the streets), comfort (by bringing lawn chairs, and so on), and enjoyment (by entertaining visitors in their homes and clubs). The Company of Neighbours spawned the reunion committee, which in turn spawned a generalized sense of commitment and responsibility that, we would argue, almost always exists in latent form among neighbours and can be energized by appropriate community activities.

Corporate organization and officially designated (professional) leadership too often remove this generalized sense of responsibility that each individual in a group must assume or reject in each situation. More than anything, that sense is the force behind our emerging theory of experiential learning in the community.

Our experiences from the reunion can offer an example. When police are in place to secure a street dance, the expectation among those in attendance is that the consequences of any anti-social behaviour will be dealt with through the force of law. Individuals at the dance may not see themselves as responsible to maintain order. However, when the state can no longer afford to 'protect' the public from itself, two options remain: eliminate public gatherings because their stability is uncertain; or allow the local groups to build solidarity and local responsibility for their activities. The reunion street dance proved that the latter option is still a possibility. We recognize that social conditions in Hespeler made this a more viable possibility than in some other places – Hespeler is not troubled by deep ethnic, racial, or class divides – but the ability of an autonomous public to be self-governing is still a heartening process to witness.

Informal Social Structures That Are 'Hardly Worth Mentioning'

As we said above, it is crucial to pay attention to the simple, unselfconscious ways in which people organize themselves for pleasurable activities, family gatherings, and celebratory events. If community developers were to study, as we did, the way in which local people gather for coffee at a preordained place at the same time almost every day, they would probably find, as we did, that the coffee drinkers say that such organizational efforts are effortless, invisible to them, and 'hardly worth mentioning.' We disagree.

More to the point for us, gatherings such as 'Tupperware parties' are more highly organized, and more intentional, than 'going for coffee.' But the companies that sponsor such gatherings have discovered that their goals can be realized by embedding the purpose of sales in an atmosphere of friendship, informality, and fun. We believe that the building of strong communities is a much more worthy goal than selling plastic containers for profit. However, not unlike Tupperware, we paid attention to the friendly, casual ways people have of organizing tasks and then sought to duplicate their familiar, informal approach.

We found that when we emulated organizational approaches that were claimed to be 'hardly worth mentioning,' people cemented relationships and accomplished tasks in an off-hand way that did not feel like work. In the process, we were able to address some of the locally defined problems and goals of Hespeler. By the same token we discovered that certain local people who had no formal standing with authorities had the credibility among their neighbours to carry out community-strengthening tasks. If the tasks are defined by the community, word-of-mouth reputation is all that is required to identify the right, skilled individual to do the job.

These people are seldom elected or appointed, nor are they designated by formal credentials. Here, for example, we think of Lary Turner, the postman who has a genius for entertainment production. His skills are not well known – 'hardly worth mentioning' in official circles – but they are known when it counts locally. This informal recognition of competence is widespread but is not applied by the state in facilitating locally motivated voluntarism in any systematic way.

The state has invested billions of dollars over the last century to educate and stabilize its population. If (as official ideology asserts) this investment was truly intended to create a democratic state, a state with individual freedom as its centrepiece, then it would make sense to work towards maximum responsibility for these educated, experienced local people, without mediating all their community activities with state/corporate organizational structures.

Leadership in communities of such highly educated people, as we enter the twenty-first century, is a fluid and multi-faceted phenomenon. In relating Hespeler's history, we have reported what we heard about the transfer of power from ruling families to the regulatory forms of the state, such as municipal governments and their bureaucracies. Ironically, the current fiscal crises of government may reverse this trend. In the current climate, self-regulation by a knowledgable citizenry in the areas of culture and community care may be the ascendant model.

The informal association of people who can make a difference is very important in times when government is intentionally undermining the foundations of the social supports provided by the larger society. When local municipal councils are centralized for fiscal reasons, when churches no longer have visitor committees because that has become paid work, then informal methods of community association might have to be brought back in order to harness the energy of communities to do increasingly necessary caring tasks. Many people are willing to do the work, but they have only small pieces of the organizational puzzle. What they often need is a mechanism to facilitate their recognition of how their piece of knowledge can contribute to the whole picture of community action. Social workers and other community educators can help with that task, but not by adhering to the professional roles they had under the outgoing state-funded system.

Our project has shown that the day has come for organizations such as the Company of Neighbours to step forward and act as a catalytic tool for communities that are ready to accept the responsibility to achieve local self-governance over culture and community care. The circumstances within each setting are of course different, and Hespeler has some unique assets that may have made things more likely to turn out well, but the principle deserves to be tried in other settings, with appropriate adjustments.

In an urban ghetto, for example, the task of recruiting local people who are known in the community and are prepared to be a force for cohesion will be very different from the recruitment that we facilitated in Hespeler. Also, the issues will be very different, with desperate, urgent needs to be addressed immediately. In an unstable, highly mobile community, the elements of 'blood, tradition, and history' will not be shared by residents at the beginning, though each person will have many stories to tell if opportunities to do so are constructed. We would expect that construction of a narrative community, and a community narrative, would still be possible in such settings. If there is little in the way of a stable social core to begin with, informally sharing personal, context-revealing narratives may help to create one over time. Such a gathering of community members, and community stories, may identify both commonalities and serious areas of difference. Further efforts at action-research are needed in order to explore the impact of our model in a more highly diverse, urban setting.

Sociological Baggage Revisited

It is important to ask again at this stage, as we did at the beginning, a question that we feel does not receive enough attention in the 'helping professions': what was in it for us? Now that the project is in local hands and the research team has disbanded, what was our own stake in the process? Did we act from some sort of charitable motives, or from missionary zeal, or were there even more selfish motives at work?

As researchers and authors, we view our engagement with community development through action-research as an important means to address our own alienation. We touched on some of these themes in the self-interview reported in part in chapter 1. Through our work, we have been able to combat our own sense of an impoverished culture of mutuality. We have been able to struggle to get back in touch with a sense of social interconnectedness that we find sadly lacking most of the time.

Though we come from very different backgrounds, both of us have turned to engaged forms of action-research in order to find the tools that could illuminate social processes that we find mysterious and/or problematic. Through our struggles, individually and together, we have fashioned a set of resources that we can apply to the task of understanding, and perhaps limiting, the over-regulation or suppression of processes that foster mutual aid in communities.

As ethnographic community developers, we wished to act not as leaders or as elite philosophizers but as well-focused mirrors. First, we reflected back to the local community respondents their statements of need and their understandings of their own milieu. Then we reflected back to them the methods of organization that they actually used to get things done. Finally, we reflected back to them their own ideas for solutions to their needs, as a way of suggesting that they had the capacity to take charge and to make the changes that they felt were needed.

The kinds of research that we have described in this work allow us to apply our education as sociologists in ways that are satisfying to us and useful to those with whom we work. Though we do not trade on our credentials in our interactions with our participants, neither do we try to adopt a false modesty as to what we can contribute. As sociologists we have been trained to identify and analyse social forms, and we have concentrated on those that we identified as having a dampening influence on citizens' engagement in community change. The insights of our instructors, and of the writers whom we have cited, have combined with our own experience, to enable us to approach this task with some confidence and to bring something of value to the endeavour.

Thus we take some satisfaction in acting on the theoretical training that we have had and in putting it at the disposal of others. The idea that there is an esoteric body of knowledge regarding community structure that cannot be fathomed by the masses is repugnant to us. As educators we see the potential for the approaches described herein to lead to the development of experiential approaches to learning in the community, approaches that are grounded in new forms of theory. We draw deep satisfaction and gratification from making a contribution to this process, but as fellow travellers, not as missionaries with a credo to spread.

Thus we close not with a profound reformulation of community within the postmodern age, and not with a new set of formulas, programs, and organizations. Instead, we offer the story of Hespeler as a community narrative and as the product of a narrative community. That story, read as a whole, carries many messages. One that we feel is clear deals more with removing the stumbling blocks of conventional social work than with erecting new programs and structures. The Company of Neighbours taught us that outside-generated, externally imposed structure impedes local autonomy and responsibility for a sustained community effort. But it also showed us that an engaged form of action-research could support that local autonomy and nurture it towards its own destiny.

The building of narrative communities is an unpredictable process, full of risk and resistant to formulation. But the story of Hespeler speaks to what can be accomplished when people undertake to use community development and action-research to construct their community narrative in a spirit of good faith and good will.

References

Alary, Jacques, ed. 1990. *Community Care and Participatory Research.* Montreal: Nu-Age Editions.

Apple, Michael. 1990. *Ideology and Curriculum.* 2nd ed. Boston: Routledge & Kegan Paul.

Armstrong, Anthony. 1977. *Masters of Their Own Destiny: A Comparison of the Thought of Coady and Freire.* Vancouver: University of British Columbia.

Aronowitz, Stanley. 1983. *Working Class Hero.* New York: Pilgrim Press.

Banks, C. Kenneth, and Mangan, J. Marshall. 1993. 'Inquiry, Education and Action: Implications for Engaged Social Research.' Paper presented at Annual Meetings of Canadian Sociology and Anthropology Association, Ottawa, Ontario, June.

– 1994. 'Researching Social Networks in Action: An Ethnographic Approach.' Paper presented at Annual Qualitative Research Conference, Waterloo, Ontario, May.

– 1995. 'Researching Social Networks in Action.' *Journal of Sociology & Social Welfare* 22, no. 3: 69–88.

– 1996. 'Facilitating a Basis for Local Progressive Change through Action-Research.' Paper presented at Annual Meetings of the Society for Socialist Studies, St Catharines, Ont., June.

Banks, C. Kenneth, and Wideman, Gail. 1996. 'The Company of Neighbours: Building Social Support through the Use of Ethnography.' *International Journal of Social Work* 33, no. 3: 317–28.

Bauman, Zygmunt. 1992. *Intimations of Postmodernity.* New York: Routledge.

Berger, Peter, and Luckmann, Thomas. 1967. *The Social Construction of Reality.* Garden City, NY: Doubleday.

Bernstein, Richard J. 1983. *Beyond Objectivism and Relativism: Science, Hermeneutics, and Praxis.* Philadelphia: University of Pennsylvania Press.

Bouchier, Nancy B., and Anstead, Christopher, J. 1994. 'From Greased Pigs to Sheepskin Aprons: Civic Holidays in Victorian Ingersoll.' London, Ont.: University of Western Ontario.

Bourdieu, Pierre, Chamboredon, Jean-Claude, and Passeron, Jean-Claude. 1991. *The Craft of Sociology: Epistemological Preliminaries*. French original pub. 1968. New York: DeGruyter.

Bowles, Samuel, and Gintis, Herbert. 1976. *Schooling in Capitalist America*. New York: Basic Books.

Braverman, Harry. 1974. *Labour and Monopoly Capital*. New York: Monthly Review Press.

Brewster, Winfield. 1934. 'The Chief Is Dead.' *Hespeler Herald*, 27 Sept.

– 1953. 'Hespeler's Heydays.' *Hespeler Herald*, 16 May.

– 1993. *La Rue De Commerce*. First pub. 1954. Hespeler, Ont.: The Company of Neighbours.

Bruner, Edward M. 1984. *Text, Play and Story*. Washington, DC: American Ethnological Society.

Burrell, Gibson, and Morgan, Gareth. 1979. *Sociological Paradigms and Organisational Analysis*. Brookfield, Vt.: Ashgate.

Campfens, Hubert. 1997. *Community Development around the World*. Toronto: University of Toronto Press.

Campfens, Hubert, ed. 1983. *Rethinking Community Development in a Changing Society*. Guelph, Ont.: Community Development Society.

Carr, Wilfred, and Kemmis, Stephen. 1986. *Becoming Critical: Education, Knowledge and Action Research*. Philadelphia: Falmer.

Carroll, William, K., ed. 1992. *Organizing Dissent: Contemporary Social Movements in Theory and Practice*. Toronto: Garamond.

Chambers, Robert. 1973. *Managing Rural Development: Lessons and Methods for Eastern Africa*. Brighton, England: University of Sussex.

City of Cambridge Archives. 1996. *Old Hespeler*. Brochure. Cambridge, Ont.: City of Cambridge Archives.

Cohen, Anthony. 1986. *Symbolizing Boundaries: Identity and Diversity in British Cultures*. Manchester: Manchester University Press.

Corbin, James, and Strauss, Anselm. 1990. *Basics of Qualitative Research: Grounded Theory Procedures and Techniques*. London: Sage.

Corrigan, Philip, and Sayer, Derek. 1985. *The Great Arch: English State Formation as Cultural Revolution*. Oxford: Basil Blackwell.

Couchman, Robert. 1986. 'The International Social Revolution: Its Impact on Canadian Family Life.' *Canadian Home Economics Journal* 36, no. 1: 10–12.

Curtis, Bruce. 1988. *Building the Educational State: Canada West, 1836–1871*. Philadelphia: Falmer.

- 1992. 'Representation and State Formation in Canada, 1790–1850.' *Studies in Political Economy* 28: 59–87.

Darnell, Regna. 1991. 'Ethnographic Genre and Poetic Voice.' In Ivan Brady, ed., *Anthropological Poetics*, 267–77. Savage, Md.: Rowman and Littlefield.

Darwin, Charles. 1989. *The Descent of Man, and Selection in Relation to Sex*. First pub. 1877. Vols. 21–2, *Pickering Masters: Collected Works of Charles Darwin*. London: William Pickering.

Denzin, Norman K. 1992. 'Whose Cornerville Is It, Anyway?' *Journal of Contemporary Ethnography* 21: 120–32.

Doré, Gerald. 1997. 'Conscientization as a Specific Form of Community Practice and Training in Quebec.' In Campfens, ed. (1997), 93–100.

Drucker, Peter F. 1993. *Post-Capitalist Society*. New York: HarperCollins.

Durkheim, Emile. 1957. *Professional Ethics and Civic Morals*. London: Routledge.

Ehrenreich, Barbara. 1997. 'Spinning the Poor into Gold: How Corporations Seek to Profit from Welfare Reform.' *Harper's Magazine*, Aug. 44–52.

Fals-Borda, Orlando. 1991. *Knowledge and Social Movements*. Santa Cruz, Calif.: Merrill.

Flynn, David. 1991. 'Community as Story: A Comparative Study of Community in Canada, England and the Netherlands.' *Rural Sociologist*. 24–35.

Foucault, Michel. 1980. *Power/Knowledge: Selected Interviews and Other Writings 1972–1977*. Brighton: Harvester.

Freire, Paulo. 1970. *Cultural Action for Freedom*. Cambridge, Mass.: Harvard Educational Review.

- 1973. *Education for Critical Consciousness*. New York: Seabury.

- 1985. *The Politics of Education*. South Hadley, Mass.: Bergin and Garvey.

- 1993. *Pedagogy of the Oppressed*. Trans. Myra Bergman Ramos, revised ed. New York: Continuum.

Freire, Paulo, and Macedo, Donaldo. 1987. *Literacy: Reading the Word and the World*. South Hadley, Mass.: Bergin and Garvey.

Frideres, James S., ed. 1993. *A World of Communities: Participatory Research Perspectives*. North York, Ont.: Captus.

Gage, Nathaniel Lees. 1989. 'The Paradigm Wars and Their Aftermath: A "Historical" Sketch of Research on Teaching since 1989.' *Educational Researcher* 18, no. 7: 4–10.

Gartell, C. David, and Gartell, John W. 1996. 'Positivism in Sociological Practice, 1967–1990.' *Canadian Review of Sociology and Anthropology* 33, no. 2: 143–58.

Giddens, Anthony. 1993. *Modernity and Self-Identity: Self and Society in the Late Modern Age*. Stanford, Calif.: Stanford University Press.

Giroux, Henry. 1981. *Ideology, Culture, and the Process of Schooling*. Philadelphia: Temple University Press.

Glaser, Barney, and Strauss, Anselm. 1967. *The Discovery of Grounded Theory: Strategies for Qualitative Research*. New York: Aldine.

Goodson, Ivor F., and Mangan, J. Marshall. 1996. 'Exploring Alternative Perspectives in Educational Research.' *Interchange* 27, no. 1: 41–59.

Gouldner, Alvin. 1976. *The Dialectic of Ideology and Technology*. Toronto: Oxford University Press.

Habermas, Jurgen. 1984. *Reason and the Rationalization of Society*. Vol. 1, *Theory of Communicative Action*. Boston: Beacon.

– 1987. *Knowledge and Human Interests*. Trans. Jeremy J. Shapiro. Oxford: Polity Press.

Haraway, Donna J. 1991. *Simians, Cyborgs, and Women: The Reinvention of Nature*. New York: Routledge.

Harvey, Percy, ed. 1966. *Hespeler Re-Union Commemorative Book*. Hespeler, Ont.: Monograph.

Hespeler Board of Trade. 1916. *Hustling Hespeler: The Town with a Future*. Hespeler, Ont.: Hespeler Board of Trade.

Hespeler, Canada: A Souvenir of the Factory Town. 1900. Hespeler, Ont.: Hespeler Herald.

'Hespeler's Founders.' 1900. *Hespeler Herald*, 8 May, 3.

'Hespeler's 100,000 Friends.' *Fergus News-Record*, 20 July 1947.

Horton, Myles. 1990. *The Long Haul: An Autobiography*. Toronto: Doubleday.

Horton, Myles, and Freire, Paulo. 1990. *We Make the Road by Walking: Conversations on Education and Social Change*. Philadelphia: Temple University Press.

Houston, Susan E., and Prentice, Alison. 1988. *Schooling and Scholars in Nineteenth-Century Ontario*. Toronto: University of Toronto Press.

Hustling Hespeler: The Town with a Future, a Good Town to Live in. 1900. Hespeler, Ont.: Hespeler Herald.

Illich, Ivan, Zola, Irving, McKnight, John, Caplan, Jonathan, and Shaiken, Harley. 1977. *Disabling Professions*. London: Marion Boyars.

Jameson, Fredric. 1991. *Postmodernism, or, the Cultural Logic of Late Capitalism*. Durham, NC: Duke University Press.

John, Lindsay H. 1994. 'Borrowed Knowledge in Social Work: An Introduction to Post-Structuralism and Postmodernity.' In Adrienne S. Chambon and Allan Irving, eds., *Essays on Postmodernism and Social Work*, 49–62. Toronto: Canadian Scholars' Press.

Kemmis, Stephen. 1995. 'Emancipatory Aspirations in a Postmodern Era.' *Curriculum Studies* 3, no. 2: 121–43.

Kemmis, Stephen, and McTaggart, Robin, eds. 1982. *The Action Research Reader*. Geelong, Australia: Deakin University Press.

Kirby, Sandra, and McKenna, Kate. 1989. *Experience, Research, Social Change: Methods from the Margins*. Toronto: Garamond Press.

Kropotkin, Peter. 1989. *Mutual Aid: A Factor in Evolution*. First pub. 1904. Montreal: Black Rose.

Kuhn, Thomas H. 1970. *The Structure of Scientific Revolutions*. Enlarged 2nd ed. Chicago: University of Chicago Press.

Laidlaw, Alexander F. 1971. *The Man from Margaree: Writings and Speeches of M.M. Coady*. Toronto: McClelland and Stewart.

Lather, Patti. 1986. 'Research as Praxis.' *Harvard Educational Review* 56, no. 3: 257–77.

– 1991. *Getting Smart: Feminist Research and Pedagogy within the Postmodern*. New York: Routledge.

Lees, Ray. 1975. *Research Strategies for Social Welfare*. London: Routledge & Kegan Paul.

Low, Jaqueline. 1993. 'Community by Association: A Case Study Comparison of Voluntary Associations with Communities Using Anthony Cohen's Theory of the Symbolic Construction of Community.' Paper presented at Annual Qualitative Research Conference, Waterloo, Ont.

Lutherwood Community Services. 1988. *Cambridge in Transition: A Look at People, Neighbourhoods and Support Services*. Cambridge, Ont.: Lutherwood Community Services and Lang's Farm Village Association.

Lyotard, Jean-François. 1984. *The Postmodern Condition: A Report on Knowledge*. Minneapolis: University of Minnesota Press.

McLaren, Peter. 1994. 'Multiculturalism and the Postmodern Critique: Toward a Pedagogy of Resistance and Transformation.' In H.A. Giroux and P. McLaren, eds., *Betwen Borders: Pedagogy and the Politics of Cultural Studies*, 192–224. London and New York: Routledge.

McLaughlin, Kenneth. 1973. *Cambridge: The Making of a Canadian City*. Burlington, Ont.: Windsor.

Macpherson, C.B. 1977. *Life and Times of Liberal Democracy*. Oxford: Oxford University Press.

McQuaig, Linda. 1993. *The Wealthy Banker's Wife: The Mulroney Government's Assault on Equality in Canada*. Toronto: Penguin Canada.

Mangan, J. Marshall. 1994. 'Using a Database Management System to Support Qualitative Research.' *Social Science Computer Review* 12: 114–21.

– 1998. 'The Watershed: New Technologies Supporting New Forms of Education.' Paper presented at Ed-Media '98, Freiburg, Germany, June.

Mannheim, Karl. 1952. *Essays on the Sociology of Knowledge*. Ed. W.J.H. Sprott, International Library of Sociology and Social Reconstruction. London: Routledge & Kegan Paul.

Marshall Macklin Monaghan, Ltd. 1967. *Hespeler Urban Renewal Study.* Hespeler, Ont.: Marshall Macklin Monaghan, Ltd.

Mills, C. Wright. 1959. *The Sociological Imagination.* London: Oxford University Press.

Mishler, Elliot G. 1991. 'Representing Discourse: The Rhetoric of Transcription.' *Journal of Narrative and Life History* 1, no. 4: 255–80.

Polkinghorne, David E. 1988. *Narrative Knowing and the Human Sciences.* Albany, NY: SUNY Press.

Prentice, Allison. 1977. *The School Promoters: Education and Social Class in Mid-Nineteenth Century Upper Canada.* Toronto: McClelland and Stewart.

Quantrell, James. 1987. 'The Economic Development of Cambridge: An Overview.' *Journal of the Waterlooo Historical Society* 75: 62–74.

Rappaport, Julian, and Simkins, Ronald. 1991. 'Healing and Empowering through Community Narrative.' *Religion and Prevention in Mental Health* 10, no. 1: 29–50.

Richardson, Laurel. 1991. 'Speakers Whose Voices Matter: Towards a Feminist Postmodernist Sociological Praxis.' *Studies in Symbolic Interaction* 12: 29–38.

Ross, Murray. 1963. *Community Organization.* Toronto: University of Toronto Press.

Saul, John Ralston. 1995. *The Unconscious Civilization.* Concord, Ont.: House of Anansi.

Scheler, Max. 1961. *Ressentiment.* Trans. W.W. Holdheim. New York: Free Press.

Scheurich, Jim. 1992. 'A Postmodernist Review of Interviewing: Dominance, Resistance, and Chaos.' Paper presented at Annual Meetings of the American Educational Research Association, San Francisco.

Schrag, Francis. 1992. 'In Defense of Positivist Research Paradigms.' *Educational Researcher* 21, no. 5: 5–7.

Scott, James. 1969. *Ontario Scene.* Toronto: Ryerson.

Seidman, Steven. 1991. 'Postmodern Anxiety: The Politics of Epistemology.' *Sociological Theory* 9: 180–90.

Selltiz, Claire, Wrightsman, Lawrence, and Cook, Stuart W. 1976. *Research Methods in Social Relations.* 3rd ed. New York: Holt Rinehart and Winston.

Shank, Richard C. 1990. *Tell Me a Story: A New Look at Real and Artificial Memory.* New York: Scribner's.

Shulman, Judith H. 1990. 'Now You See Them, Now You Don't: Anonymity versus Visibility in Case Studies of Teachers.' *Educational Researcher* 19, no. 6: 11–15.

Simon, Roger, and Dippo, Donald. 1986. 'On Critical Ethnographic Work.' *Anthropology and Education Quarterly* 17: 195–202.

Spring, Valeries. 1986. 'Cute as Buttons.' *Cambridge Archives*, 19 Dec., 16–17.

Tesch, Renata. 1990a. 'The Art of Coding Qualitative Data: How to Develop an Organizing System.' Paper presented at Annual Meetings of the American Educational Research Association, Boston.

– 1990b. *Qualitative Research: Analysis: Analysis Types and Software Tools.* Philadelphia: Falmer.

Trillium Foundation. 1995. *In Search of the Civil Society: The Trillium Foundation Annual Report for 1994–95.* Toronto: Trillium Foundation.

'Union Notes.' *DW&W News*, June 1943.

VanManen, Max. 1990. *Researching Lived Experience: Human Science for an Action-Sensitive Pedagogy.* London, Ont.: Althouse Press.

Wagner, Jon. 1993. 'Ignorance in Educational Research: Or, How Can You *Not* Know That?' *Educational Researcher* 22, no. 5: 15–23.

Walker, Gillian. 1990. *Family Violence and the Women's Movement.* Toronto: University of Toronto Press.

White, Michael, and Epston, David. 1990. *Narrative Means to Therapeutic Ends.* New York: W.W. Norton.

Willis, George. 1991. 'Phenomenological Inquiry: Life-World Perceptions.' In Edmund C. Short, ed., *Forms of Curriculum Inquiry*, 173–86. Albany, NY: State University of New York Press.

Winter, Richard. 1987. *Action-Research and the Nature of Social Inquiry.* Brookfield, Vt.: Avebury/Gower.

Index

CPSIA information can be obtained
at www.ICGtesting.com
Printed in the USA
BVHW032117130422
634248BV00018B/84

9 780802 079053